Music Is the Key

Music Is the Key

to unlocking your child's potential

Karen O'Connor

Best Wishes
Karen

LONDUBH BOOKS

First published in 2012 by
Londubh Books
18 Casimir Avenue, Harold's Cross, Dublin 6w, Ireland
www.londubh.ie
1 3 5 4 2
Origination by Londubh Books; cover by sinédesign
Printed by ScandBook AB, Falun, Sweden
ISBN: 978-1-907535-27-7

We are all made to shine as children do…It's not just in some of us. It's in everyone.

Marianne Williamson, *A Return to Love: Reflections on the Principles of A Course in Miracles* (1992)

Dedication

I now know that the essence of an excellent therapist, doctor, teacher or clinician is is their passionate belief that there is a way to make things better and in believing there is a way they are creating the way. I wish you the joy of knowing and working with someone like this.

Contents

Acknowledgements

It was a real eureka moment for me when I started to see that not just one child but every child was making great progress using music. It was then I knew I was on to something big and that I had to tell the world. To my mind the best way to let the world know about the power of music and these life-changing techniques was by writing a book.

This sent me on a journey to Toronto to talk to Paul Madaule – author of *When Listening Comes Alive* and creator of the Listening Fitness Programme (LiFT™) – to see what he thought. We spoke at length and Paul was so encouraging and supportive and excited at the prospect of my writing a book that I felt confident that this was an important thing to do.

However it was really the next morning when I was leaving Toronto that I got the confirmation I needed. I flagged down a cab outside the hotel to bring me to the airport and was chatting with the taxi driver when out of nowhere he said, 'My father gave me a really unusual name. You'll never guess what it is?'

I made a few attempts but didn't come close. 'I give up,' I said.

'I knew you'd never guess,' he laughed triumphantly. 'My name is Amadeus.'

So a special thank you to Wolfgang Amadeus Mozart not only for giving me a lift to the airport but most importantly for inspiring me to write this book.

There are so many exceptional people I want to say a special thanks to. First and foremost the beautiful children with whom I have had and continue to have the great pleasure of working and playing every day. You never cease to amaze and delight me and teach me something new every single day. Thank you.

Thanks to my friends and family for all your love, support and encouragement. You have inspired me to be who I am. I couldn't have done it without you.

To the great team, past and present, that I have worked and work with – Fidelma, Susan, Áine and Carmel. You inspire me on a daily basis. An additional thank you to Carmel, who was the first person to edit my book. What great courage and patience you have.

Thanks to the great therapists, clinicians, teachers and doctors with whom I have worked and learned over the past seventeen years.

Particular thanks to Dr Goodwin McDonnell, Andrea McDonnell, Helen Brennan, Paul Madaule, Morana Petrovski, Sheila Frick, Terry Fahy, Eileen Dwyer, Pauline Moran, Karen Clancy and Bernadette Molloy.

To other exceptional people with whom I have not had the pleasure of working but would dearly love to have worked: Wolfgang Amadeus Mozart, Jean Ayres and Dr Alfred Tomatis.

All brilliant in their own right, they had this quality in common: they were never happy to stick to tried and tested methods but searched endlessly for groundbreaking techniques and tools that would change the lives of individuals for ever, enhancing their talents and helping them achieve their true potential.

I now know that the essence of an excellent therapist, doctor, teacher or clinician is is their passionate belief that there is a way to make things better and in believing there is a way they are creating the way. I wish you the joy of knowing and working with someone like this.

Thanks to the people who believed in me and brought this little baby on its last and critical step so that it could be born into the world – my friend and adviser, Rose, my adviser, Terry Prone, my publisher, Jo O'Donoghue, my chief publicist and great friend, Orla Collins, and my sub-editor and great friend, Ann

Brehony.

I love you all.

Thank you.

Karen O'Connor, Galway, February 2012

Introduction

'Music is the key to unlocking your child's potential,' the therapist said with conviction.

As a consultant speech and language therapist with years of experience, I thought I was hearing things. But what if it was true? What if listening to Mozart and other classical composers could help a child to be calm and focused, to understand better, to speak more clearly, to engage more effectively, to interact and to learn? What a difference it could make to children, changing their lives forever: enabling them to create better friendships and better relationships and achieve a better standard of education. Maybe at last there was a way to ensure that our biology did not need to dictate our biography.

I thought of all the children I was working with and how, although they were improving to a degree with conventional speech and language therapy techniques, they were not achieving their true potential. They needed something more. Could listening therapy be the missing piece of the jigsaw? I wondered if this new tool could bring children with challenges further, helping them to achieve their full capabilities. Years later, having used these techniques with thousands of children with many different diagnoses, I know that everything I heard that day – and so much more – was true.

I was listening to Sheila Frick, an occupational therapist and expert in the field of sensory integration. She was explaining to a room full of European therapists and clinicians how the most talented and experienced American therapists were incorporating auditory interventions and sound therapies into their practices, with exciting results. She explained how auditory interventions, such as Therapeutic Listening® and the Listening Fitness programme (LiFT™) could dramatically affect a child's neurology by impacting on the neuroplasticity of the brain and in so doing could help that child to make extraordinary progress, improving skills that are imperative to a child's development, such as the ability to be calm and focused; to pay attention and listen; to concentrate; to develop fine and gross motor skills; to develop comprehension and expressive language skills; to play appropriately; to develop social skills, self-esteem, confidence and the ability to learn.

If it was true, it could mean that children would achieve results in weeks rather than years, allowing them reach their true level of ability fully rather than partially.

Over the years many parents have asked me: 'What led a senior speech and language therapist to incorporate sound therapy into her practice?'

What really brought me to that room that day to learn about listening techniques and sound therapies?

Having worked for many years in a variety of settings with children with many different diagnoses that ranged from specific language impairment to speech and language delay to autism to dyspraxia and everything in between, I was aware that although children's skills were developing they were often not achieving their potential. When I worked within the public health service, I struggled with the practice of discharging children when they reached a certain level of development that often fell far short of their individual potential. As therapists we knew there was nothing more we could do with our conventional speech and language techniques.

However, it was frustrating, as a determined therapist, to be told to discharge children at this stage, knowing that they still required intervention. I knew there had to be another way. There had to be other tools that we could add to our speech and language therapy tool kit, to help children achieve their true level of ability. With this in mind I went in search of other approaches and techniques that could help children. My journey brought me all over the world, introducing me to the most talented, innovative therapists and the most gifted children.

The journey really began with my first speech and language therapy manager within the public health service, who introduced me to the concept of sensory integration. From day one, she gave us as speech and language therapists the sense that we had a role to play in combining sensory integrative techniques to help children achieve their communication potential. She encouraged us to attend sensory integration courses and to use the skills we learned to help the children we worked with progress even further. We learned how to use sensory integrative techniques to work on developing the sensory skills at the lower levels in order to facilitate the spontaneous emergence of skills at higher levels.

Jean Ayres, a Californian occupational therapist and pioneer in the field of child development, created the whole concept of sensory integration theory and practice. She described in detail how successful integration of sensory information including auditory (hearing), tactile (touch), visual, gustatory (taste), vestibular (movement) and proprioceptive (movement of the muscles and joints) at the brain stem level (level one) leads to the emergence of age-appropriate motor and attention skills (level two), facilitating development of age-appropriate speech and language skills (level three), and ultimately learning and social skills (level four).

Ayres described speech and language difficulties as a symptom of underlying sensory processing and integration difficulties at the brain stem level, rather than difficulty higher up in the brain. She proposed treating the underlying sensory processing difficulty, to allow the brain to integrate the information more effectively so that skills could be acquired naturally. This type of therapy would also lay the foundations for more spontaneous, independent development of skills at higher levels. By refining the foundation senses – auditory, vestibular, proprioceptive, tactile and visual – we are enhancing the way children process and integrate information at the brain stem level. This treatment will support and enhance the emergence of skills at higher levels of neural development, much like a domino effect.

Harvard psychiatrist Dr John Ratey noted that the opposite is also true. He highlighted that any difficulty integrating sensory information can lead to a cascade of events resulting in challenges in many areas, including regulation, attention, motor, language, learning and self-esteem. I often explain to parents that the processing and integration of sensory information at the base of the brain is like building the foundations of a house. If the foundations are not solid, you can do all the work you want on the walls, the windows, the door and the roof – the house will never be adequately supported. Similarly if the brain is not processing and integrating sensory information effectively at the base level, the child's skills will not develop as they should at the higher levels of the brain.

I have worked with many exceptional occupational therapists who have developed Jean Ayres's approach. Their in-depth knowledge of the body and the ways in which it lays the foundation for speech and language development is fundamental for speech and language therapy to be most effective. In order to develop each child's potential, speech and language therapists should have a basic understanding of how the body lays the foundation for the head, moving from gross to fine skills, developing the gross motor skills first in the body and later the finer motor skills required for the consistent development of speech, language and learning.

The body can tell us a great deal about the child's speech and language development. Canadian psychologist Paul Madaule describes this phenomenon by using the analogy of a camera on top of a tripod. The body is like the tripod and the camera is the head. If the tripod (the body) is unsteady due to issues like pronounced or even subtle coordination difficulties, it will make the camera (the head) unsteady also, leading to the picture being out of focus and shaky. This will result in the poor development of attention, speech and language and motor, social and academic skills. However, by looking at the child holistically and realising that speech and language difficulties do not happen in a vacuum, we learn that body awareness, coordination and balance come first and that speech and language come as a result. It makes sense that speech and language therapists should work closely with their occupational therapy colleagues, developing an understanding of how one area impacts on the other and in doing so dramatically improve assessment and treatment protocols and practices. A psychologist colleague of mine in New Zealand also suggested that 'all child psychologists should have an understanding of sensory integration to ensure that they diagnose and treat children in the most effective way.'

So how do we as therapists treat underlying sensory processing difficulties effectively?

I had been using simple sensory integrative techniques that I had learned and was seeing some improvements in the children as a result but I thought there had to be more effective ways of impacting directly on the nervous system. Then I attended my first listening course with Sheila Frick and was introduced to the fascinating world of listening techniques and sound therapy. She spoke of Alfred Tomatis, the French ear, nose and throat consultant who was the founder of sound therapy. He was the son of an opera singer and his father referred many of his opera colleagues who were experiencing vocal problems to him. Tomatis soon found traditional treatments inadequate in treating his patients and came to realise that many vocal problems were actually the result of hearing problems.

Tomatis proposed the tenet: 'The voice does not give what the ear does not hear.' He adapted his techniques very effectively to target many language and learning disorders, recognising that the role of the ear went beyond hearing.

I was hooked.

I began to attend more listening therapy courses, combining my new-found knowledge of specific auditory interventions such as Therapeutic Listening®, advanced Therapeutic Listening®, Samonas Sound Therapy and the LiFT™ programme with my knowledge of speech and language therapy. And so the journey began for all involved: for me, for the children and for the families. We learned together and worked together, watching each child's skills emerge, and we saw every day that when we incorporated music and sound-based techniques into the children's speech and language programme, they began to fly, finally beginning to achieve their true potential. Seventeen years later I can say that I've never looked back – and neither have the children. Seventeen years of experience have shown me that sound therapy and other sensory integrative techniques are the best way to treat the foundations of the house (bottom-up approach) and speech and language techniques are the best way to fix the roof (top-down approach).

As a colleague pointed out to me quite recently, I'm in a unique position, having spent the first six years of my working life using conventional speech and language therapy techniques and the last eleven years combining auditory intervention techniques with speech and language therapy strategies. I have amassed many years of experience working with thousands of children with a variety of different diagnoses, watching their skills unfold, layer by layer, first sensory, then motor, followed by speech and language, and ultimately social and academic. This experience has convinced me of the efficacy of sound-based therapy. As founding director of the Listening Therapy Centre, Ireland, a highly successful centre of excellence to which hundreds of families travel every year, I can say with my hand on my heart that there is no comparison between what can be done with auditory interventions and what can be done without them. It is imperative that sound-based techniques be incorporated into each child's speech and language therapy programme to maximise their outcome. Music truly is the key.

The world of sound therapy is very much alive in the USA, Canada, Australia and New Zealand. It is encouraging to see that a growing number of health and education professionals are beginning to incorporate sound-based techniques into their own practices here in Ireland. I have incorporated three techniques into my own practice, the Listening Therapy Centre, with remarkable results. By combining traditional with more innovative techniques, I am seeing children achieve their attention, motor, communication and learning potential in a dramatically shorter period of time.

I felt compelled to write this book to let families know that there is a bright light at the end of the tunnel. Innovative techniques are available to help children unlock their capabilities – and in my experience Therapeutic Listening® and the LiFT™ programme are two of the best. The following stories emphasise the importance of incorporating sound-based intervention techniques into speech and language therapy.

By writing this book I wanted to give parents hope: hope that each child can achieve his or her own true potential, whatever level that is. Let me show you how I did it, through a number of stories about amazing children with whom I have had the great pleasure to work.

1

Michael: the engineer who couldn't plan...yet

(Clinical diagnosis: Asperger's Syndrome)

Michael was literally sitting on my doorstep when I returned from the first listening course given by Sheila Frick in London in 1999. What a picture he painted there on the doorstep; gangly and tall for his age, with short blonde hair and an intense, almost agitated look in his blue eyes. We often joked about that later: how important it is to use 'soft eyes' when interacting with people. It certainly was a lot less intimidating. His mum was standing there beside him, talking to him with a worried look on her face.

I had met Michael and his mum a number of years earlier when he came to see me when I worked in the child psychiatry department of the public health service. At that point I used speech and language therapy techniques only, as I was not trained in any form of auditory intervention. Now here we were again, three years later, but this time combining auditory interventions with speech and language therapy techniques.

Sheila Frick's words rang in my head: 'I have one wish for you: that you may be lucky enough to find your first ten listening clients respond exactly as I have described: that they will teach you so much about using auditory interventions that when a more complex child comes along you will know exactly what to do.'

I could not have been luckier than with Michael. Although he was quiet to begin with, as we moved through the Therapeutic Listening® programmes we started to see his true personality emerge. And what a character he was, full of fun and jokes. He came from a big family and his siblings and parents had the incredible knack of always seeing the funny side of life. He was a perfect first listening client because he responded exactly the way I had hoped to the different music, making all the expected changes. He was able to listen to the music for the suggested amount of time and all we saw were improvements and changes such as I had never seen before. I was so excited as I wondered if I had found the missing piece of the jigsaw. I now see these changes with children on a daily basis but at that point I had never seen anything like it. Still, no matter how many times I see a child progressing and developing, it never ceases to astonish and delight me.

Michael was nine years of age and had a diagnosis of high-level autism when we first met. However, I always believed he was much more like a child with Asperger's Syndrome. He had the desire to interact and engage with others; he just did not know how to do it. It did not matter what I did, or what tool I pulled from my speech and language repertoire, nothing seemed to engage him sufficiently to allow him to make any real progress. His major challenges at that point were in the areas of: a) attention and regulation; b) auditory processing and comprehension; c) expressive language; d) motivation to interact and engage with others; and e) complex two-way communication and social skills in general.

His parents were concerned about his poor attention, his limited ability to understand or use language and his poor interaction with others. His original language assessment took place in May, 2000. We used the Clinical Evaluation of Language Fundamentals – Revised UK (CELF-R UK) language assessment, the most detailed language assessment available, which looks at six areas of language; three relating to comprehension and auditory processing (receptive language) and three relating to expression (expressive language). Michael scored below average in three of six areas assessed, covering both receptive and expressive language skills. He achieved an age equivalent of seven years and two months although he was nine at the time.

Looking at his results in more detail indicated that Michael had a moderate receptive and expressive language disorder, or specific language impairment, as it is often termed. In *Communicating Quality*, which outlines standards of good speech and language therapy practice, speech and language disorder is defined 'as a disorder in children who are not acquiring speech and/or language skills in accordance with an age-appropriate developmental pattern or sequence'. For Michael these scores meant that his language and learning were almost two years behind his peers so at the age of nine, he was functioning more like a seven-year-old.

However, no quantitative assessment that involves ticking boxes and scoring can truly describe the extent of Michael's difficulties and how they were impacting on his life. Indeed, from a quality of life point of view, he had a limited attention span and he was highly distractible. His ability to understand and retain what teachers, peers and parents were saying was poor, as was his ability to express himself verbally.

'How could he have any friends?' his mum wondered sadly. 'He can't understand what they are talking about. He can't converse with them.'

When Michael attended regular speech and language therapy with me several years earlier, we had used a variety of techniques and approaches. We worked on an individual basis and in small groups. For example in our social skills group, I found myself constantly asking him if he was listening: he always looked as if he was not, even when he was. We did everything we could to encourage Michael to listen and attend better, to develop his awareness and to encourage better self-monitoring, using everything from role-playing to videotaping. But his listening was so poor and he was so distractible that he was unable to pay sufficient attention to allow him to process the auditory information given in order to express himself fluently. We achieved little if any progress.

When I combined speech and language techniques with auditory interventions this was a totally different experience for both of us. When we started Michael's Therapeutic Listening® programme, I gave his mum the equipment along with his detailed individual therapy plan and arranged to meet them three weeks later. I designed a programme specifically to work on building Michael's skills in accordance with his natural development. I selected music from the Therapeutic Listening® range called 'Ease #1', that would incorporate the significant contrast between foreground and background sounds with high and low frequencies. I expected this to exercise his middle ear muscles, which would help with his general sensory regulation and ultimately improve his attention and listening skills. The second piece we introduced was called 'The Sounds of Nature', which was designed to improve spatial awareness, knowing that this was a big issue for Michael because of his poor eye contact and poor coordination through space. This piece can be extremely helpful for individuals who lack a solid understanding of three-dimensional space.

I met Michael and his mum three weeks later but was completely unprepared for what was to take place. The changes I saw in Michael were dramatic. At the beginning of each session, I would encourage Michael to draw, which helped him to relax. It also allowed me time to observe changes in his skills, including his body awareness, spatial awareness and self-awareness, which is so often apparent in drawings. Michael loved to draw in the most intricate detail. At that time, I worked from home in an office upstairs at the front of the house. A building was being constructed across the road, which could be seen clearly from where he used to sit. He was fascinated by that building and drew it on many occasions.

We began the session, as normal, with a drawing. However instead of drawing the building across the road, Michael turned towards me. Looking straight at me, as if seeing me for the first time, he began to draw me.

I knew this was the beginning of great things for Michael. It may seem insignificant but to me it was tangible evidence that sensory integration was taking place. The initial piece of music, 'Ease #1', had helped to lay the first critical foundation; Michael was calmer, more regulated and listening better. Then 'The Sounds of Nature' had introduced the next beautiful layer, which enabled Michael to localise sound more easily in space. His own awareness of the space around him and where he was in relation to other people and objects was starting to evolve. Now that Michael had a better idea of where he was in space, he had a reference point with which to find other people, allowing him to make eye contact, interact and engage. Steve J. Cool, Professor of Neurobiology in Pacific University, Oregon, describes this most effectively in his analogy of shopping malls in the States. In each mall there is a map to help you work out where you are, so that you can then locate the different shops in relation to your position. Without the red dot that says 'You Are Here', it would be impossible to locate any other position on the map. Strangely enough, I once had this experience in an American shopping mall, while looking desperately for a particular shop. Unfortunately the map did not have the 'You Are Here' dot and, try as I might, I could not work out how to get to the shop I wanted. I could see the shop on the map but because I was unable work out where I was in the shopping mall space, I could not find it. If your body does not understand space how can your brain understand it? This sense of spatial confusion leads to difficulty understanding and mastering spatial concepts such as in, on, under, behind, beside, and later the more complex concepts of first/last and before and after.

Michael made real progress with each new Therapeutic Listening® programme, which helped him to come together step by step. We know from the work of Cutler, Stevens-Dominguez et al (1992) that there are three levels or orders of regulation in the brain. The first level begins early in infancy when the organisation of autonomic nervous system function, such as breathing, temperature, sleep-wake patterns and muscle tone, take place. The second level strategies are also developed in infancy when the child's brain begins to organise skills such as sucking, swallowing and breathing, often referred to as the suck, swallow, breath synchrony (SSB). The child also learns to vocalise in more organised patterns and can focus on visual and auditory information in a more developed way. It's at the third level of regulation that skills come together to enable the child to plan, sequence and be organised in all areas, developing the ability to understand and put language together and to plan and organise the body to go to the other side of the room. However, it is important to know that levels one and two are fundamental for the development of level three. In Michael's case I could see that he was now much more organised at levels one and two, which laid excellent foundations for the development of level three skills. In real terms this meant that he was calmer and more regulated, so his attention was better. Once his attention was better, his listening improved and his comprehension developed as a result.

'He's asking so many questions,' his mum said exasperatedly 'He never really went through that stage. It's driving us crazy but it's great.'

Michael was expressing himself more, using much longer, more organised sentences. His improved spatial awareness formed a solid base for his enhanced localisation of sound in space, resulting in better processing of auditory information for understanding. Proper spatial awareness gives us our reference point, allowing us to locate other people and objects in space, laying the groundwork for looking, watching, engaging, interacting and, ultimately, developing better social skills.

Over a six-month period I had seen more changes in Michael than I would ever have thought possible. There was no comparison between the progress we had achieved using

Therapeutic Listening® and the limited progress we had made with traditional speech and language therapy techniques. The changes were dramatic, improving areas that I could not have reached with traditional speech and language therapy techniques alone: areas like attention, regulation and the desire to interact and engage. These improvements in Michael's sensory integration in turn allowed him to benefit fully from standard speech and language interventions.

Then I came to a point where, although Michael had reached a good level, I knew he was capable of further development. I knew the LiFT™ programme would bring Michael to the next level in his development, so I spoke to Michael and his mum about the benefits of the programme. They had witnessed such good progress with their home programme of listening that they were motivated to try something more intensive like the LiFT™ programme.

Michael started to make changes quickly once we started the LiFT™, particularly in attention, concentration, comprehension, expressive language and academic and social skills. All his skills were developing further, reaching much higher levels: levels we had originally thought Michael could not achieve. It is strange working with children: certain incidents, particular things they say or do, will stick in my mind. There were many such incidents with Michael. I suppose the first was when he drew my picture instead of sketching his favourite building. The second was when we began phase two of the LiFT™, during which period he read into his microphone for two half-hours a day. During this time, the children are actively encouraged to read and talk. One day Michael was reluctant and I remember insisting that we needed to do some more reading.

'I don't want to read,' he shouted at me angrily. 'I just want to talk to you.' I sat with my mouth open, unable to respond. I thought it was an astonishing reply for a child who had such challenges engaging and interacting with people, a child who originally appeared to have no real desire to talk to anybody. Here he was almost demanding interaction from me in annoyance. This was another turning point.

His mum happily told me he was having arguments with his brothers for the first time. She also remarked that he was much funnier than she had noticed before. It was not just that he understood and enjoyed his siblings' jokes and pranks; he was starting to play a few tricks of his own. A new awareness both of himself and of others was emerging. He was developing the skills not only to understand others but to express himself. He was no longer passively going along with what his brothers and sisters decided; he had his own opinions.

Some relatives of Michael's family had recently come home on holiday from the US. They went out for dinner one night and his mum sat amazed, listening to Michael initiate a lively discussion about American presidents and politics. His relatives, who visited every year, were astonished and could not believe the difference since the previous year.

I formally assessed Michael on three occasions over the entire period of his therapy; once before we started treatment, the second six months later and the third at the end of therapy, four years later. When I initially assessed Michael, although he was nine, he was scoring more like a seven year old. After a six-month period of sound therapy his scores had improved dramatically, by two years and seven months. That was great progress in only six months. I continued to develop Michael's skills using a combination of Therapeutic Listening® and the LiFT™ programme over the following months and years. Then, at the end of therapy, I reassessed Michael. He was then thirteen years old but came out at a language age of sixteen years and five months. This was impressive progress.

These results proved what Sheila Frick had always said: that this form of therapy could indeed change children's lives for ever. At last children could achieve their full communication and learning potential. I no longer needed practically to stand on my head to find ways to help Michael to progress.

The cold facts of test results can never adequately show how much Michael's quality of life changed. He was transformed from a young boy who took little notice of his siblings and peers into a teenager who interacted more fully with his peers and argued with his siblings. He began to make friends for the first time, even inviting some of them over to his house. He wanted to go into town at lunchtime with them and he spent three weeks with his best friend in a residential French summer college 150 kilometres away from home.

Michael's story proved to me the undeniable benefits of incorporating sound-based techniques into a child's speech and language therapy programme. His success marked the start of a great journey for both of us. Little did we know it would change our lives; Michael's life was enriched because he was now able to see, understand and interact with the world in a better way; my working life was enhanced because I had at last found a tool that could help children truly achieve their individual potential.

2

Theo: the astronaut who couldn't understand space...yet

Clinical diagnosis: autism or dyspraxia, with underlying sensory integration dysfunction

I first heard about Theo from a former colleague. She wanted to refer a little guy to me because she was moving back to Australia. She described a three year old who might have not just speech and language difficulties, as originally thought, but autism. Theo's parents did not agree with the autism diagnosis, as they explained that he was much more interactive at home. However they did have concerns about his poor attention, comprehension and listening skills. They were worried about his inability to put words together, his limited play skills and his lack of engagement and eye contact.

When I first met Theo, he wasn't even as tall as the half-door of my thatched cottage. He arrived with his worried parents, his mum holding his thin little hand tightly. They were friendly and chatty but he was very quiet. He didn't say a thing. He was a cute little guy with the palest skin and pale blue eyes with dark circles under them. How disconnected he was, not looking at anyone or focusing on anything. When he arrived and his mum introduced him, I knelt down in front of him so that he could see me clearly but even then his eyes were everywhere except on me.

I was immediately struck by how 'lost in space' he appeared. He had that kind of 'woozy' look in his eyes, like a child who was dizzy from spinning too much. This was an immediate indicator to me that his vestibular and proprioceptive systems were not processing information correctly. The vestibular and proprioceptive senses are often referred to as the 'overlooked senses' but in terms of normal function they are as important and often more important than the other senses. The vestibular sense tells you which way is up: how your body is oriented in relation to up and how your body is moving in space. It's constantly giving us important information about where we are in space, our sense of spatial awareness, our balance, posture and the coordination of the two sides of our bodies. It also has an impact on how alert we feel and it regulates our moods. This is all essential information in terms of functioning effectively in the world.

The vestibular system is a fluid-filled cavity located in the inner ear, comprising a semi-circular canal-type structure. It works closely with the proprioceptive sense. This sense, often referred to as the sixth sense, tells us where our body is in space and controls different parts of the body. When proprioception is intact and processing information the way it should, a child can, for example, walk downstairs with ease. However when a child's proprioceptive system is not processing information effectively they will struggle to know where they are on the stairs, how far from the top and, more importantly, how far from the bottom they are. They will often compensate by relying on their visual sense to give them this information about how to get up and down those stairs. Any distortion or interruption to the correct flow of information from these two senses will lead to a variety of developmental problems for a child.

When Theo first came in, he did not explore the treatment room at all; instead he fell from one activity into another. In fact he was so 'lost in space' that he could not recognise who or what was in the space around him and if he did happen to encounter another person, he was unsure of how to interact across the space between them. He found it difficult to interact and engage and his play skills were limited. His eye contact was so poor that I could not as yet decipher whether his lack of engagement was due to spatial issues or an absence of motivation. I often use a smaller room to assess children because the restricted area is less stressful for them, providing more defined boundaries: this allows for a more genuine indication of the child's skill base. However, I always make sure to observe children across a variety of spaces: entering the building, in the small clinic room and in a larger clinic room, to establish if they react differently in different-sized spaces.

I decided against a formalised assessment at my first meeting with Theo, as his ability to pay attention to a task was so poor. However we gathered important information from more informal assessment, combined with clinical observations of Theo and detailed discussions with his parents. This information highlighted that his ability to communicate, interact and engage was significantly better, more natural and more spontaneous when he was in a more confined space. It was like a revelation to me when he climbed into a cardboard box, which happened to be in the treatment room. Well, in truth, he almost fell into it. Once he was inside, however, everything changed. He was noticeably calmer. The box appeared to provide Theo with the sense of containment he needed, the boundaries he needed to determine where his body was in relation to the size of the space he was now occupying.

Once he had a better sense of the details of the space around him, I began to glimpse Theo's real potential. His play changed immediately and he began to verbalise a little more. He engaged in less sensorimotor play, displaying more mature symbolic play and, most importantly, he started really to connect with me. (Sensorimotor play is a typical form of play for children up to the age of two, in which children experiment with sensation and movement, whereas symbolic or make-believe play is much more imaginative and generally peaks at four to five years of age.) This was a very different little guy from the one who had walked in my front door half an hour earlier.

Theo's mum laughed nervously. 'I didn't think to mention it, Karen, but he loves getting into small spaces,' she said. 'You could find him anywhere, under the kitchen table, in the cupboard, under his bed, behind the curtains.'

When I observed Theo inside the box, I saw that his eye contact was better, his interaction was more effective and it seemed as if he was better able to connect with people around him. These inconsistencies encouraged me to believe that there was a lot more this little guy could do, once his difficulty with his sense of space had been resolved. His attention was still limited; he moved frequently between various activities and toys. I tested Theo's receptive language skills (his level of understanding) using the Derbyshire Language Scheme Play Test. He was able to understand at a one-word level: for example he responded correctly to, 'Give me the cup,' or, 'Give me the teddy.' This is more consistent with what you would expect a twelve- to eighteen-month-old child to do than a three-year-old.

However, the natural and spontaneous interactions Theo exhibited at times indicated that there was a high possibility of a different diagnosis here – not autism as had been suggested but much more likely dyspraxia with underlying sensory integration difficulties. Children who have autism and children with dyspraxia with underlying sensory integration difficulties can often demonstrate similar traits, particularly in the early years. It is vital that every professional assessing children should have a good understanding of sensory integration and its impact, as this would prevent a lot of misdiagnosis in this area.

When assessing a child, it is important to consider the child holistically, looking at all the pieces of the developmental jigsaw to work out what is going on and why. This kind of holistic assessment allows us to implement the most effective treatment programme, one that is individually tailored to each child. When I assess a child, I often feel like a detective as I try to decipher the clues to what is happening, what is working well or not working so well and what key pieces of the jigsaw are missing or compromised in some way. In my experience, most children have all the pieces of the jigsaw but they just cannot put them together to complete the full picture. When the pieces are not working together well this can make the child appear 'out of sync' with the world and the people in it, as described by Carol Kranowitz in her book *The Out of Sync Child* (1996).

What are the pieces of the developmental jigsaw?

A good sensory profile combined with a detailed developmental history and clinical observations will provide a lot of information about a child. In Theo's case it was obvious that things were not quite as they should be with his sensory integration development. He was certainly 'lost in space', which indicated that his vestibular and proprioceptive sensory systems were not correctly processing information about space and his body's movement through space. I could not decide whether Theo's poor eye contact, lack of interaction and engagement were due to a more pervasive developmental delay, an underlying sensory integration dysfunction, or a combination of the two. I hoped that it was an underlying sensory integration dysfunction because if this was the case, I could pull Theo's jigsaw together quickly and help him to resolve most of his challenges within six to twelve months. There certainly were strong indicators of sensory integration dysfunction: poor processing of vestibular and proprioceptive information such as that 'lost in space' look in his eyes, as well as poor awareness of how to move effectively through space, which was characterised by lots of tripping over objects on the floor. Theo was also finding it difficult to process low frequency sounds. His parents described how he would run out of the room when the hair dryer or the vacuum cleaner was turned on.

His dad said nervously: 'You're not going to believe it but the sound that he's really afraid of is the hand dryer. He nearly loses his life when he sees it, never mind hears it.'

I did believe it.

Theo's difficulty in processing spatial information was presenting itself as an auditory defensiveness. Older children who have difficulty processing low frequency sounds (not to be confused with a hearing difficulty) describe how they are unable to localise the source of the sound. They explain that they cannot work out where the sound is coming from in space. They feel as if the offensive sound is all around them and coming down on top of them. This can be quite frightening; hence their often exaggerated reactions to such a sound.

Low frequency sounds are those below 1000 hertz, which contain limited spatial information. Any child who has difficulty processing these sounds may have either a tactile defensiveness (sensitivity to touch), because low frequency sounds actually touch the body, or poor spatial awareness (difficulty processing spatial information), or a combination of the two. It made more sense, given the picture of Theo that we was developing, to conclude that he had difficulty with the latter.

Theo's social and academic profile looked something like this:

Social and academic

- poor eye contact
- poor interaction and engagement
- limited awareness of where others are in space and how to engage across a space
- poor learning

Speech and language

- poor localisation of sound in space
- poor understanding of language
- limited expressive ability
- poor planning of sentences

Attention and motor skills

- limited attention span, easily distracted
- poor spatial awareness
- poor planning and sequencing ability

Sensory integration

- poor vestibular processing
- poor proprioceptive processing
- auditory defensiveness

As the pieces of the puzzle came together, it was becoming clear that it was Theo's underlying sensory processing and integration difficulties that were causing the motor, attention, speech, language and social difficulties further up the line. But I wondered if there was an additional social piece that was unrelated to his sensory integration challenges.

It was time to put the pieces of Theo's assessment jigsaw together and begin the most effective treatment programme for him. I spoke to his parents at length and recommended that we commence a home programme of Therapeutic Listening®, combined with a basic home programme of speech and language activities. I knew that if things were quite different when I saw him some weeks later the diagnosis would not only be much clearer but that it would be more indicative of dyspraxia with underlying sensory integration difficulties.

Theo returned to the clinic six weeks later quite a changed child from the one I had seen at the initial assessment.

'He's like a different child,' his mum smiled happily. 'Now I know he's not there yet but at least I can see him improving. I didn't see any change at all with the work the other speech therapist was doing. So this is progress.'

I could see it the minute he walked in the door. He made eye contact with me straight away and was making more regular eye contact with his mum. He was calmer, more focused. He was beginning to understand where he was in space and as a result the world was starting to make more sense to him. He was more vocal, using many more single words and, most importantly, he was trying to engage and interact more. The diagnosis was becoming clearer: dyspraxia with strong underlying sensory integration difficulties. The Therapeutic Listening® programme we had put in place had been developed to improve his ability to process and integrate sensory information more effectively and as a result the real Theo was beginning to appear.

It wasn't only Theo who was changing. I could see his parents looking less drawn and nervous and much more excited and hopeful about their son's future.

Week by week we watched Theo progress in many areas. We met once a month over a four-month period, adapting his Therapeutic Listening® programme while blending in speech and language activities. We began to see changes in his ability to regulate himself: he was calmer, listening and understanding better. He developed a bigger vocabulary of single words and began to make attempts at two-word phrases, for example 'Mammy gone', and 'Bye bye, Daddy.' He became clearer and more articulate. His play developed from simple sensorimotor, to include more complex symbolic or make-believe elements.

Theo's desire and ability to interact and engage were also growing and developing and, most importantly, he was connecting. His parents were excited about the improvements and I knew it was time to look at introducing a more intensive sound therapy programme – the Listening Fitness Programme (LiFT™). The LiFT™ is a thirty-day intensive sound therapy programme that generally takes place in the clinic. It is split into two fifteen day phases; the first fifteen days being the receptive phase and the second fifteen days the expressive phase. Within two days of starting the LiFT™, Theo became quite 'disregulated', a term therapists use to describe how the child can become out of sync when many changes are taking place. His parents were worried but I reassured them this was a sign that he was sensitive to the music and would begin to make changes quickly. Children may become disregulated during the LiFT™, because their perceptions are changing and being reorganised in a better way. Once the changes have integrated into the child's nervous system they will become regulated again but by then lots of significant changes will have taken place.

Big changes came with the first LiFT™. Theo's difficulties were reducing and his understanding of space was developing; he was conquering and understanding space like never before. And then he took off. Everything became a vehicle to navigate and move through space. Boxes of all shapes and sizes became rockets, planes, even elevators. He wanted to engage with the other children on the programme to help him bring his big plans to fruition. Every day he had lots of ideas about what to create and how to create it. He had his team of workers in place and took every opportunity to direct them. They flew aeroplanes and launched rockets to the moon, taking in the planets in the solar system, each flight involving intricate spatial planning.

Many of those journeys were accompanied by emotional outbursts and tantrums. The other children were not always willing followers of Theo's grand scheme and this often led to mutiny among his fellow astronauts. But with the mutiny came social learning: how to negotiate, how to reason, to engage with and motivate the others to become part of his team. Theo's vocabulary exploded because he was now highly motivated to put his words together to engage and organise the troops in the pursuit of his master plan. His language became more complex, with longer utterances and improved vocabulary. He began to ask questions that, although beyond his language ability, were in line with his overall cognitive ability. He asked about God and how he was born and where he came from. He wanted to know how electricity worked and where water came from.

A six-month period of Therapeutic Listening® followed,

during which Theo refined his skills. He was doing well but I could see that we weren't quite there yet and that I had more to do to help him achieve his potential. I discussed with his mum the benefits of doing a LiFT™ Boost programme. This is a ten to fifteen day programme, combining the receptive and expressive phases over a shorter, more intensive period, and is suitable for individuals who have progressed on the full LiFT™ programme. My aim with the LiFT™ Boost was to augment Theo's skills in all areas in order to have him functioning naturally at a higher level. I believed his spatial awareness, his receptive and expressive language, his concentration, attention and social skills would improve, impacting positively on his social and academic performance.

Again he became somewhat disregulated during the programme, but much less so than before. This was to be expected as his perceptions were improving quickly but as a consequence they were in a state of flux. Working with programmes like Therapeutic Listening® and the LiFT™ is like unfolding the brain. This type of therapy works precisely on the areas experiencing difficulty, opening up the neural pathways and facilitating the previously stifled natural developmental pattern. Because of the brain's neuroplasticity (ability to reorganise itself to accommodate newly acquired skills), the music and more specifically the frequency changes within the music impacts on the nervous system at each level of progressive neural development. Theo was making dramatic progress in all areas, including his ability to remain calm and focused, his spatial awareness and his language and social skills.

I reviewed Theo as normal six weeks after the end of the LiFT™ Boost programme. I undertook a detailed language assessment and the results were exactly what I would have expected. Theo's language scores were all age-appropriate and even above his age in some areas. Great progress. Theo was at last achieving his true potential.

I continue to review Theo once a year to ensure that all is going well. His parents are very excited about his progress. Theo is now attending mainstream primary school, without any need for additional assistance. His teacher is pleased with his schoolwork.

'There's nothing to worry about with Theo,' the teacher said with a laugh one day. 'If they were all doing as well as him, my life would be easy.'

Theo has turned a major corner. If his sensory integration problems had not been picked up he could have been completely misdiagnosed as having autism. I see so many children with exactly the same profile of difficulties as Theo, some to a greater or lesser degree. Children like Theo show us how important it is to look at each child holistically, with an in-depth understanding of how sensory integration difficulties can impact on their development in many areas. This understanding will, at assessment level, lead to a more accurate diagnosis and in turn to the most effective treatment programme.

Children's drawings of a person

Many therapists/clinicians use children's drawings of a person as part of their assessment. These drawings can reflect a child's development in a number of areas: perceptually, intellectually, physically and emotionally.

Therapists interested in sensory integration also consider how these drawings demonstrate body scheme, a sensorimotor map of one's own body in relation to space. Having an accurate body scheme underlies the development of praxis (the ability to conceive of, plan and execute a series of coordinated body movements). In his book, *Children's Drawings as Diagnostic Aids* ((1970), Joseph H. Di Leo describes how drawings may be considered expressive of change in a child himself.

Drawing 1: Prior to the beginning of the LiFT™ programme

Theo's first drawing was on the day he came to the centre, two weeks before his first LiFT™. This is what he drew when I asked him to draw a man. As you can see it is extremely difficult to work out what the drawing represents. His mum said that this was typical of any drawings he did, although he didn't draw very much at all.

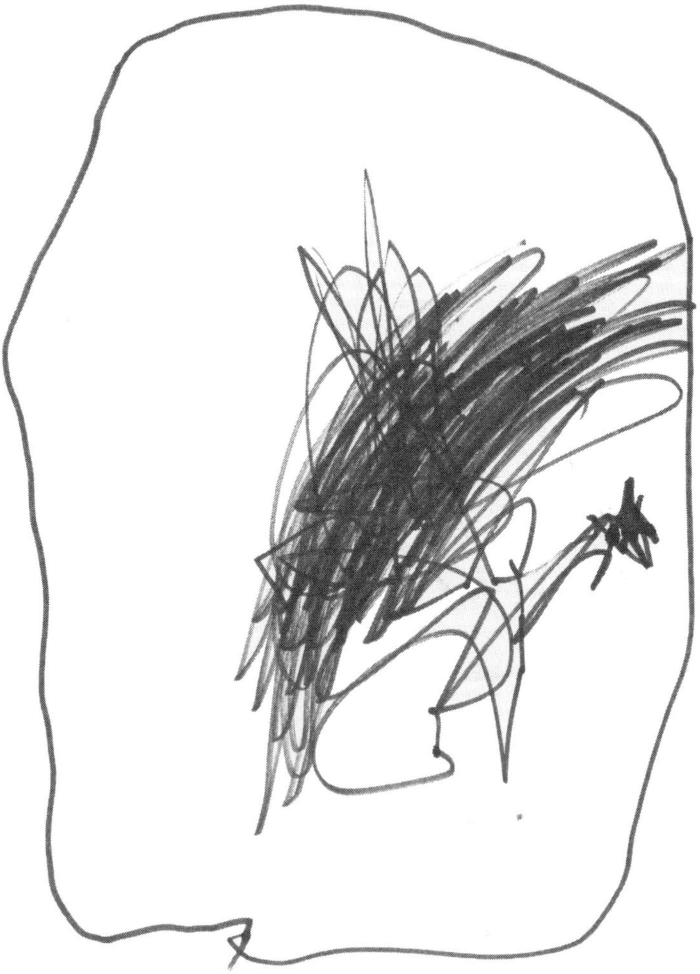

Drawing 2: Five days into the LiFT™ programme

Theo's drawing of a man is changing. It's starting to take shape: the eyes, nose, mouth and hair are becoming clearer and are all in the area of the face. The legs are separate and below the face as they should be.

Drawing 3: Day 10 of the LiFT™ programme

This drawing clearly shows a person, with the head and body represented separately. The eyes and hair are also clearly shown. Overall the drawing is much more refined than previous drawings and much more typical for Theo's age.

Drawing 4: Day 14 of the LiFT™ programme

Theo's final drawing during the first fifteen days of the LiFT™ programme is a much more complete representation of a person, with the head and body shown separately in a more three-dimensional manner.

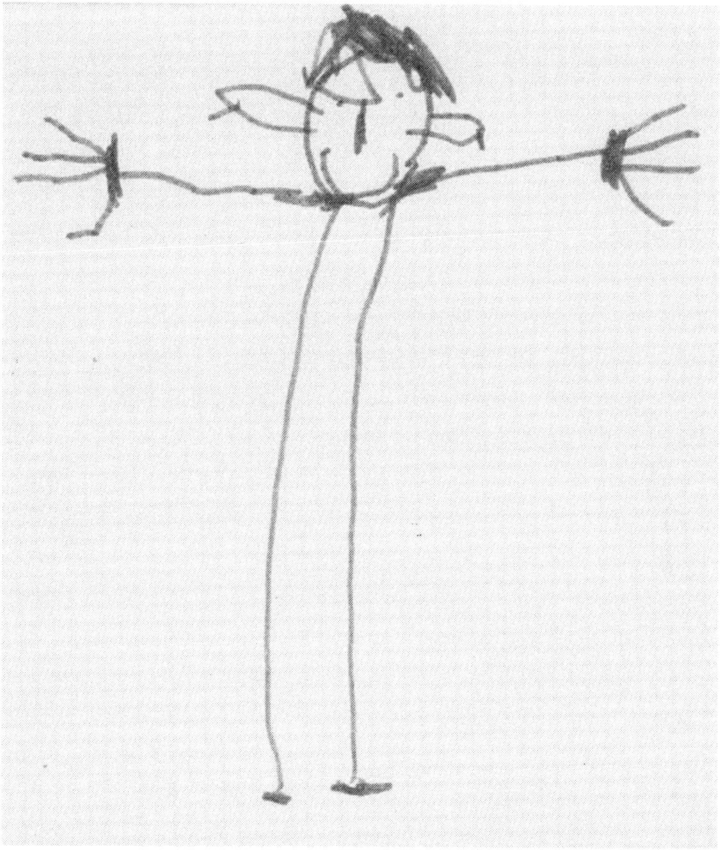

3

Raphael: the playwright who couldn't play...yet

Clinical diagnosis: autism

I meet many parents who believe their child will not be able to do this or achieve that, all because professionals have told them so. There are parents who fear their child will never go to a birthday party, have a friend or get married. While, of course, it is important have realistic expectations for our children, often a diagnosis can dictate expectations that are too low and consequently the child falls far short of the level they could achieve. My job is to help the child achieve their true potential, no matter what the diagnosis is. Just because your child had a difficult start or was given a very negative diagnosis doesn't mean there is no light at the end of the tunnel.

We now know that with the right input a large number of diagnoses and disorders need no longer have the negative impact they once had. Many conditions can be improved significantly using listening therapies such as Therapeutic Listening® and the LiFT™ programme. My experience demonstrates that the best results will be achieved by using listening therapies combined with speech and language techniques to help children achieve their true level of ability. I always say to parents that we will work together to help your child achieve his own potential, whatever that is, and in my experience this place is always better than where the child was when I first saw him.

I remember the first time I met Raphael. He was just five

years old, a miniature version of his dad; well-built but quite chubby, with short black hair that was spiked on top. He looked like butter wouldn't melt in his mouth but, boy, did he have his dad wrapped around his little finger! I will never forget his dad's first words to me: 'I'm sure there's nothing that you can do but I wanted to bring Raphael anyway as a last resort,' he said sadly.

'That's why my wife didn't come with me today,' he explained later. 'She couldn't face being told nothing else can be done to help.'

Raphael is a prime example of a child whose potential was being underestimated and who, as a result, was not making progress. I engaged with Raphael from the minute he came in the door and started to notice lots of interesting things about him. I already had a detailed developmental history that Raphael's parents had sent prior our first meeting but you can tell a great deal about what is happening by observing a child, particularly in a new environment.

Raphael had poor eye contact. Although he would look at me, he would then look away quickly, which made me wonder if he had some type of visual defensive or visuomotor difficulties. He was putting two words together at times when interacting with his dad: for example, 'Daddy sit,' or 'Daddy stop.' This type of phrase formation was quite delayed for his age, being more typical of a two year old than a five year old, and is often a real indicator of planning and sequencing difficulties. His articulation was poor but I was encouraged to see that there was some nice two-way interaction going on with his dad.

It was Raphael's mum who made the initial telephone referral; she explained that he had a diagnosis of autism. Their primary concern was in the area of speech. It remained a major problem, causing Raphael a lot of frustration and leading to behaviour problems. He had received sporadic speech and language therapy through the public system. However, when Raphael's mum requested more input the therapist said, 'He has autism. More speech and language therapy is not going to make any difference. You just have to accept it.'

We sent detailed questionnaires to Raphael's family, which helped us to gather a comprehensive birth, sensory, motor, communication and learning history. Raphael's mother had a normal pregnancy and birth. He had a history of ear infections with bilateral grommets inserted at the age of two. He did not crawl but bottom-shuffled instead. He was walking at sixteen months and talking at two years old, using only a few words, and was slow to put words together. There were some important early indicators in his history that point to later development of speech and language difficulties. A strong history of ear infections can lead to attention, listening and comprehension difficulties and also have an impact on expressive language difficulties. This was certainly true in Raphael's case. The fact that he did not crawl and was slow to put words together were also early indicators that his brain had difficulty in planning and sequencing. Of course planning and sequencing ability impact on the development of a wide range of skills such as planning of play, speech, language and how to interact. Planning and sequencing difficulties are underpinned by poor sensory processing and difficulty integrating sensory information. These early processing difficulties would have compounded any difficulties he might have been experiencing and put him in a high-risk category for listening, attention, speech, language and learning difficulties.

Other important early indicators of later speech and language difficulties are:

1. Prematurity

In my experience children born prematurely can have a variety of speech and/or language difficulties. Twins and children of multiple births, who may have been induced pre-term, also tend to have planning difficulties, which are initially obvious in movement and later in language. The child often presents with expressive language formulation issues, which may include difficulty putting words together into sentences and thinking of the exact word he wants to use.

2. Poor early sucking and feeding

This can be a strong early indicator not only of feeding difficulties but of later speech difficulties. The muscles used for sucking and feeding are also used for speech production. Early difficulty coordinating sucking with swallowing and breathing, as in the suck, swallow, breath synchrony, and organising the muscles of the mouth for effective planning and organisation, can in many cases lead to speech difficulties (Oetter et al, 1995).

3. A failure to crawl

I have seen failure to crawl or possibly crawling for a limited period and/or using walkers or other walking aids exacerbate planning difficulties. Crawling represents one of the first big opportunities the brain has to plan; if the child does not crawl, it is often an indication that the brain is unsure how to plan and sequence. I have commonly seen this impact on the development of planning and sequencing for the production of language.

4. A history of ear infections

A history of repeated or significant ear infections can impede the effective working of the middle ear muscles, which can lead to difficulty with listening, attention and processing of auditory information contained in sounds and words.

In Raphael's case, the fun started once we sat at the table to look at some assessment materials. He engaged intermittently with the materials and stopped regularly to look back at his dad, as if he was on the verge of giving up, before suggesting McDonald's.

'I'll bring you to McDonald's if you work for Karen,' his dad promised, hopefully. Raphael returned to the activity we were doing. Five minutes later I could see his head turning, slowly but surely, in the direction of his dad. With a twinkle in his eye he looked at his dad and started to move away from the table.

'Don't forget McDonald's,' his dad said a little uncertainly. 'I'll buy you chicken nuggets...and chips.'

Still nothing. Raphael kept moving and kept his eye on his poor dad at the same time.

'And...I know your mother doesn't allow it but I'll get you a McFlurry's, just this once,' his dad almost pleaded.

Bingo! Raphael was back in his seat again and doing his work.

What great skills of negotiation and manipulation Raphael had. He hardly had to say a word but, through non-verbal communication, he said everything. All in a day's work for Raphael. There was a lot more to him than met the proverbial eye.

It was this exchange that made me realise how capable Raphael was in terms of social interaction and engagement but also in terms of 'theory of mind'. Theory of mind is a specific cognitive ability that enables a person to understand what other people know, think or feel. Raphael's ability to read his dad's expressions and understand what he was thinking and feeling was excellent. It was obvious that his ceiling of skills was actually high and that with the right level of motivation he could reach them. We just needed to achieve this level of motivation all the time without having to resort to McDonald's.

Let's look at the pieces of his jigsaw:

Social and academic

- limited social interaction
- underachieving at his specialised pre-school

Speech and language

- poor understanding of language
- poor planning of language

Attention and motor skills

- clumsy
- poor crossing of the midline
- mixed laterality

Sensory

- poor vestibular, proprioceptive and tactile processing
- low to average muscle tone

Raphael's parents gave information in Raphael's sensory profile that highlighted his vestibular, proprioceptive and tactile processing difficulties. Raphael's low to average muscle tone predisposed him to having poorer sensory processing, which could lead to poor motor, speech and language, attention and social development. His parents indicated that he was the only one of their children who disliked the playground. He might go on the slide but would not go on any of the other pieces of playground equipment. He often became upset and cried to leave. How a child copes in the playground tells a lot about that child's vestibular system as each piece of playground equipment stimulates the vestibular system, some to a greater and others to a lesser degree. The up and down motion involved in the slide is probably one of the least stimulating to the vestibular system, whereas a child swinging quite high is probably one of the most stimulating.

In terms of the tactile sense Raphael disliked washing his hands and face and could become disruptive when his teeth were being brushed. There were no current problems with wearing different types of clothes, though there had been in the past. Raphael sought lots of horseplay, much more so than his brothers. Dad reported that it often become way too rough for his brothers and even for him at times.

Movement

Informal observation of Raphael's movement highlighted difficulty with jumping, hopping and skipping. His parents noticed that he was quite clumsy and often tripped over objects on the floor. Looking at this area gave me important information about the foundations of Raphael's speech and language development. I also referred him onward to an occupational therapist for a more in-depth assessment of his motor skills.

Speech and language assessment

I undertook a comprehensive range of speech and language tests and the results showed that Raphael's comprehension and ability to express himself were significantly below average.

Looking at his speech highlighted immaturities in his production of words, as opposed to any specific difficulties.

By looking at Raphael from a sensory integrative perspective, I could see more clearly what was happening and plan the most effective form of treatment. I saw that his speech, language and motor difficulties were a symptom of underlying sensory processing difficulties. If I could make an impact on Raphael's underlying sensory processing difficulties, using a bottom-up approach (working on the foundation of the house; the real cause of the difficulty) and also a top-down approach (using speech and language techniques) I felt confident that we would see much bigger changes.

Following a three-hour assessment, the comprehensive treatment programme I developed for Raphael comprised:

- a Therapeutic Listening® programme
- a sensory diet of activities including deep-pressure oral massage and the Wilbarger Protocol (DPPT: Deep-Pressure and Proprioceptive Protocol) Both these programmes work on helping the tactile sense process and integrate information much more effectively.

- a speech and language therapy home programme

I reviewed Raphael's programme four weeks later. His parents had noted positive changes in the areas of regulation, attention and comprehension. Ongoing assessments and clinical observations supported these findings. Raphael continued to follow a Therapeutic Listening® programme for six months and I reviewed it once a month.

At this juncture I knew that he was ready to commence a Listening Fitness (LiFT™) programme, which would bring him to the next level of development in a number of key areas: attention, comprehension, expressive language, interaction, engagement and learning.

So we embarked on Raphael's first LiFT™ programme. All went well for the first few days, but then he went haywire, as his mum said. He kicked the car door, whereas previously, even at his worst, she said, 'He would have never done that.' However, within a few days everything calmed down and I started to see some positive changes. Periods of disregulation that take place during the LiFT™ are short-lived, happening at times when the brain is mastering new skills, and are followed by the emergence of a new, higher level of skill.

As part of the LiFT™ programme I sometimes introduce puppetry with children who are ready to develop their symbolic play further. Raphael did not want to engage with the puppets and he became quite upset about it. Was this an indicator of his level of symbolic understanding or was it due to his difficulty processing proprioceptive information? I thought the latter was much more likely, as he had a similar response to clowns and even to his parents wearing glasses. In my experience children with proprioceptive difficulties often have poor visuospatial processing skills and as a result find it difficult to make sense of what they see, particularly if something or someone looks different from the norm.

I reviewed Raphael six weeks after the end of the LiFT™ programme. His parents confirmed that all the improvements that had begun to take place during the programme had developed much further and that the negatives had gone. Raphael's attention and comprehension had improved significantly but he now had obvious difficulty with 'wh' questions. His sentences were increasing in length and complexity; we needed to work on developing these even further. Raphael's ability to interact and engage was also becoming more complex but he needed lots of practice with this. A speech and language therapy programme was put in place to focus on all these areas. Raphael's eye contact had not improved at all. I liaised with Raphael's occupational therapist about this and she put a specific visuomotor programme in place for him. We also referred Raphael to an ophthalmologist in the local hospital, who identified visuomotor difficulties: difficulty organising the eye muscles for specific eye movements. The ophthalmologist put a specific programme in place to encourage Raphael to practise and develop specific eye movements.

As Raphael was working on his visuomotor programme we reintroduced a Therapeutic Listening® programme to support and enhance further his emerging skills. This focused specifically on the development of his speech, language and social skills. His programme was reviewed once a month and at each review his mum would describe his progress with pride. She described how Raphael had changed from being a child who had regular meltdowns, when friends upset him, to being a resilient child who could remain calm and argue his point. We used to laugh because Danny, a particular friend of Raphael, who seemed to be very streetwise, became our gauge for how well Raphael was doing socially. As Raphael's mother used to say: 'There is no better test than out on the road with the other kids.' His mum told me that his language and social skills had developed so much that he teased, laughed and argued with his five brothers. He was making good progress.

Six months later Raphael had continued to refine his skills and I decided that a fifteen-day LiFT™ Boost programme would be beneficial. This is a ten to fifteen-day sound therapy programme that I developed for him to incorporate both the receptive and expressive phases over a shorter period than the standard LiFT™. One year later Raphael had attended two LiFT™ Boost programmes and continued Therapeutic Listening®, combined with speech and language therapy and regular occupational therapy in the interim periods.

Raphael no longer meets the criteria for a diagnosis of autism. His most recent language assessment using the *Clinical Evaluation of Language Fundamentals* (*CELF*) 4 UK reveals age-appropriate scores on all core language tests. He is doing well academically to the point that his classroom assistant is no longer necessary.

'There's one thing that's quite different about Raphael from the other children in his therapy group,' the occupational therapist commented to his mum one day. 'His social skills are definitely much better than the other children but it's not just that – they're just so natural.'

Ironically, after Raphael's difficult introduction to puppets and the world of symbolism, he now writes, produces, directs and sometimes even stars in his own plays and stories.

Overleaf are some examples of Raphael's stories:

The King.

Look at the king. He cannot sing. He gives the queen a ring. They are on the swing. The king and queen are Looking for dimonds.

Super

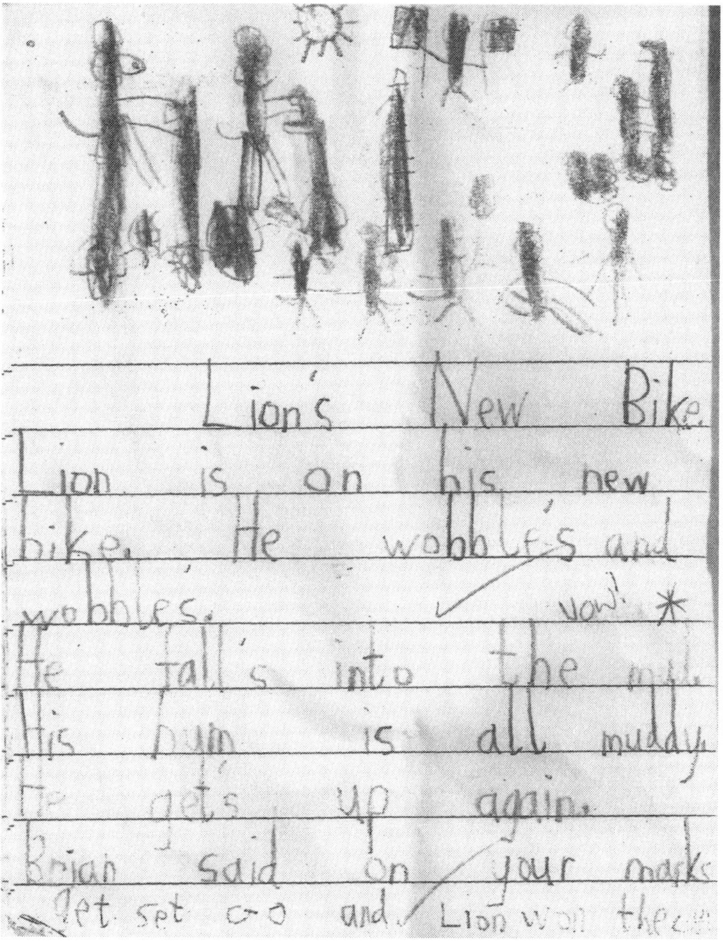

Lion's New Bike.

Lion is on his new bike. He wobble's and wobbles. vow! *
He fall's into the mud.
His bum is all muddy.
He gets up again.
Brian said on your marks get set go and Lion won the

Raphael's potential was completely underestimated. As a result he was not progressing, to the point that even his parents were giving up hope. Recognising his potential was the first step in moving him towards his true ability. He needed auditory interventions combined with speech and language therapy and occupational therapy to help him realise his true ability and to prove that his biology did not need to determine his biography.

'I don't know what you're doing with Raphael,' the school principal said after Raphael's first LiFT™ programme, 'but whatever it is, keep doing it. He's flying it.'

4

Nathaniel: the politician who didn't know how to talk ...yet

Clinic diagnosis: speech and language delay with early stammering

Nathaniel was a fun little guy of four. He was small and stocky, with dancing green eyes. He was such a little character and always made it his business to stop and chat to people, even when he couldn't say very much. He was very sociable and interactive, which made him seem older than his years. I think the phrase 'he's been around before' was created for Nathaniel. He was referred to me originally with a diagnosis of mild to moderate speech and language delay.

At the initial assessment it was obvious that Nathaniel had indeed a mild to moderate speech and language delay and that he also had a moderate stammer. The professional standards for speech and language therapists determine that 'a speech and language delay exists when a child's speech and language skills are being acquired in accordance with known developmental patterns but are delayed for their age'. They define dysfluency or stammering 'as a disorder which affects the fluency of speech production or the smooth flow of speech. Disorders of fluency are usually characterised by overt features, for example, repetition of sounds, words or phrases, and sometimes covert features, for example, avoidance behaviours and feelings of anxiety.' Guitar (1998) describes stammering 'as an abnormally high frequency or duration of stoppages in the forward flow of speech'.

I had no major concerns about Nathaniel's speech and language skills, as I knew I could develop them quite easily, blending traditional speech and language therapy techniques with a home programme of Therapeutic Listening®. However I did have concerns about his lack of fluency. Was I going to be able to help Nathaniel become 100 per cent fluent?

I created a home programme of listening to develop Nathaniel's attention and listening skills. This also focused on developing his ability to process information auditorily and to express himself verbally. I did not want to work directly on Nathaniel's speech delay at this point, as I was concerned that it would draw his attention to his speech in a negative way and as a result exacerbate his stammering or dysfluency. By working on Nathaniel's other skills through his listening programme we were able to develop the skills that would support and enhance his ability to speak more fluently. My theory was that if Nathaniel's expressive language improved and had more of a flow to it, he wouldn't hesitate to such a degree when trying to plan out sentences and that this would ultimately support and enhance his fluency.

Using a Therapeutic Listening® programme in this manner was highly beneficial as it meant I could develop Nathaniel's language skills in an indirect manner, without Nathaniel even being aware of it, so that it didn't exacerbate his stammering. Over a three-month period, Nathaniel's expressive language skills began to develop considerably: his sentence length increased from two-word phrases, for example, 'Mammy gone,' to five-word sentences like, 'Mammy is gone into town.' However, although Nathaniel's language skills were developing at a dramatic rate and becoming much more age-appropriate, his stammering persisted.

We needed to look more closely at the possible causes of his dysfluency. It is accepted within the world of speech and language therapy 'that children can be born with a predisposition to stammering, possibly inherited, and then other factors will influence when and how it emerges and how it develops. These factors are broadly divided into four categories: physiological, linguistic, environmental and emotional factors' (Rustin, Botterill and Kelman, 1996):

1. Physiological factors may include a family history of dysfluency, gender and a faster rate of speech. Stammering is more common in boys than girls and generally runs in families. However there was no family history of dysfluency in Nathaniel's case and his rate of speech was typical for his age.
2. Linguistic factors often include delays in speech and/or language development. This was certainly a factor for Nathaniel and we were using the Therapeutic Listening® to develop Nathaniel's speech and language skills indirectly without drawing his attention in any way to his speech or to language difficulties.
3. Environmental factors may include competing with a sibling or siblings to speak, or periods of difficulty or change either at home or at school. These were not factors for Nathaniel. His family was supportive and relaxed about his fluency and had not drawn his attention to his dysfluency in any way.
4. Emotional factors: 'can include sensitivity, tendency to worry or set high standards' (*Afasic Glossary*, 2004). These emotional factors were not relevant to Nathaniel as his mum described him as 'an easygoing, fun little guy'.

Therefore of the four categories of factors that are known to impact on the emergence and development of stammering, only one applied to Nathaniel: he had a speech and language delay. But his speech and language delay was improving dramatically so why was the dysfluency or stammering persisting? This was the question going round and round in my head. I began to think there must be another reason, factor or variety of factors that caused his dysfluency to persist.

Interestingly, the research has shown that approximately 5 per cent of children between the ages of two and six can experience periods of non-fluency or stammering. Research also indicates that approximately 80 per cent of children will achieve normal fluency with or without help. Children can stumble when learning to walk and trip when learning to run; so too can children stammer when learning to talk. A young child is generally unaware of the difficulty they are experiencing and of course this is the ideal time to knock the dysfluency/stammering on its head. When a child becomes more aware of their difficulty, it can lead to increased anxiety and exacerbate or prolong the dysfluency.

At this point I began to incorporate another approach to address Nathaniel's dysfluency indirectly. Using Ann Irwin's excellent book, *Stammering in Young Children*, I began to work directly with Nathaniel's parents and preschool teacher to increase their awareness and understanding of stammering and ultimately to put strategies in place to maximise fluency. This helped to a limited degree.

We also introduced breathing and breath support strategies to optimise the length and quality of Nathaniel's breath for speaking. Again we made limited progress, which wasn't consistent and didn't generalise or carry over the way I would have hoped. I didn't want this little guy to become aware of his dysfluency as I felt it would lead to the emergence of secondary behaviours, which could cause the stammering to continue and possibly intensify. We needed to help Nathaniel to be much more fluent before we could progress with any direct speech and language work.

The question went around in my head again. There must be another factor or variety of factors that can cause dysfluency to develop. Apart from the range of well-known and widely accepted causative factors already outlined, I have noted others over the years, for example: a) low/low to average muscle tone: Nathaniel presented with low to average muscle tone, as reported by his occupational therapist; b) delayed early motor development: Nathaniel's occupational therapist also indicated that his early motor development had been delayed; c) poor emergence of laterality (the ability of one side of the body to emerge as the dominant side, something that can take place only when the two sides of the body are working well together): Nathaniel presented with a weakly established laterality; and d) history of ear infections: Nathaniel had no history of ear infections

We found that we could tick three of these four causative factors and, interestingly, all three related to Nathaniel's body.

This was it. This was the key. Leonardo da Vinci's words came back to me. I needed to pay attention to the 'intelligence of the body'. I needed to look at Nathaniel's body to understand what was happening with his speech and more specifically what was causing his dysfluency.

If we look more closely at the factors listed above, we see that Nathaniel presented with low to average muscle tone. This impacts on all the muscles, including the middle-ear muscles; the malleus, incus and stapes. If the middle-ear muscles aren't working as quickly and efficiently as they should be, it can be difficult for the ears to work well together and they need to work well together so that one ear can emerge as the dominant or lead ear. The French doctor and auditory specialist, Alfred Tomatis, concluded 'that a weakly established lead ear was often associated with speech, language, reading and learning problems'.

Nathaniel's occupational therapist explained how low to average muscle tone also predisposes a child to having poor early motor development. Initially the two sides of the body need to work well together so that one side emerges as the dominant or lead side: hand dominance, foot or eye dominance and, most importantly for speech, ear dominance. When I looked at Nathaniel's body I could see that the two sides of his body were not working particularly well together. For example, Nathaniel found it difficult to jump with his two feet together, hopping was difficult for him and skipping was out. In fact, any activities involving bilateral integration were impossible for him.

When I looked at how Nathaniel's laterality was emerging I could see that he had an unestablished laterality: informal testing indicated that his left hand was emerging as the dominant hand although parents and siblings were all right handed. His mum reported that he had been quite slow to decide which hand to use predominantly. He had continued to use both hands until quite recently and would still at times use either his right or his left hand. He appeared to be right foot dominant. However he couldn't decide which eye to use to look through the telescope and instead put it between his two eyes.

I have seen this many times with children with poorly established eye dominance. They find it difficult to isolate one eye because a lead or dominant eye has not emerged. When I watched Nathaniel speak I could see that the same thing was happening but this time with his ears. His hesitations and repetitions of sounds and words were all indicators that he didn't have a lead ear.

This suggested that Nathaniel's two ears were not working well together. If the two sides of the body aren't working well together one side cannot emerge as the dominant or lead side. It seemed that dominance had not emerged correctly in the right ear. Early in his work Alfred Tomatis identified the 'lead role' of the right ear in the control of the voice. Paul Madaule (1999) explains in his book, *When Listening Comes Alive*, that Tomatis realised that a weakly established lead ear was often associated with speech, language, reading and learning problems. He proposed that the left ear simply didn't seem to have the same quality of control.

According to Madaule, Tomatis felt that the importance of the right ear as a lead ear may be related to where our heart is located. His proposition was that the left recurrent nerve that connects the brain with the larynx has to make a detour, whereas the right nerve follows a much more direct and shorter path. Most nerves leading from the brain cross to the other side of the body: for example the left side of the brain controls the right side of the body. Thus the left side of the brain is connected to the right side of the larynx.

Madaule continues: 'once children emit their first sounds, they realise that not only can they perceive sounds but they can also monitor them. Children begin to play around with sounds, the ear picks them up and then they repeat them again.' This sound-play 'is the beginning of attuning the auditory zoom to their own voice. As the child's voice control becomes more precise – when the zoom is attuned enough, the sounds are only repeated twice, e.g. ma-ma, da-da, pi-pi –the babbling phase of language development.'

Madaule explains: 'Tomatis believed that this double response was nothing more than the neural impulse coming from the brain to the larynx at two different times. Therefore the ear-to-brain-to-larynx-back-to-ear control loop is more direct for the right ear, as the right recurrent nerve is shorter. If all goes well, the right ear becomes the leading, the listening ear.' Tomatis proposed: 'that if for some reason the right ear is not in a position to assume this control, it will either be picked up by the left ear or a listening dominance may not take place at all.' Therefore there will be no lead ear. In both these cases, hesitant and monotonous speech may occur, possibly stammering or stuttering – all because the right ear didn't develop as the lead ear.

It was clear that we needed to help Nathaniel's two ears to work together first, so that his right ear could emerge as the dominant ear. This, I hoped, would result in close to 100 per cent fluency. I discussed my theory with Nathaniel's mum. She was interested and I recommended the LiFT™ programme as I believed that this was the answer. The receptive phase would help to fine tune Nathaniel's ability to process sounds and words correctly and clearly. The expressive phase would build on this, developing Nathaniel's ear-voice connection. The combination of the two phases would finally help Nathaniel's two ears work together so that a lead ear could emerge, thereby dramatically improving his fluency.

About the same time, his mum received an assessment appointment with a speech and language therapist working in the public health system. 'He's ready for direct work on his speech,' the therapist explained.

'But won't that make him more aware of his stammering and possibly make it even worse?' Nathaniel's mum replied.

'Not at all,' the therapist asserted. 'If anything his speech will be clearer and that will help him to be more fluent.'

Nathaniel's mum was understandably confused and concerned. Alarm bells went off in my head. Nathaniel was at a vital stage. I knew that any direct work on his speech at this point would not only exacerbate his fluency difficulties but ensure that it became a longer-term issue. I rang his speech and language therapist to discuss my concerns about working directly on his speech when he had fluency issues and suggested that he attend a specific fluency programme with them instead, something like the Lidcombe programme. (This is an early stammering intervention in which parents are trained to optimise their child's fluency using specific techniques, including giving positive verbal responses when the child achieves fluency.) The therapist explained that there wasn't a Lidcombe available at that time. She had already offered Nathaniel a number of appointments and wanted to begin direct speech work with him as she felt it was the best treatment for him.

I got a call from Nathaniel's mum two weeks later. 'He's much worse,' she cried down the phone. 'What am I going to do? He can hardly get a word out without stammering?'

'Stop the direct work on his speech immediately,' I replied. 'That will take the pressure off him and he will become more fluent.'

Nathaniel's mum decided to stop the speech therapy. We discussed where to go from there. At this point Nathaniel's language comprehension and expression were age-appropriate but his speech development continued to exhibit particular difficulties such as: a) fronting: when sounds which should be produced at the back of the mouth are produced further forward in the mouth, for example cat -> tat, car -> tar, cap -> tap, game -> dame, gate -> date; b) cluster reduction: when the speaker omits one of the two or three consonants that occur together; for example: 'black' becomes 'back' and 'sweet' becomes 'weet'; c) stopping of fricatives, when long fricative sounds (f, v, s, z, sh, th) are produced as short plosives (p, b, t, d, k); for example: 'sunny' is produced as 'tunny' and 'fish' is produced as 'pish.'

Although Nathaniel continued to exhibit these speech difficulties, he was not yet ready to work on this area. There was plenty of time for that later. It was his fluency that we first needed to establish firmly.

We started the LiFT™ and I was hopeful that by the end of the thirty-day programme Nathaniel would be much more fluent. He was hesitating less and getting stuck on sounds and words much less frequently. But I wasn't prepared for what happened. By the end of week one of the LiFT™, Nathaniel was significantly more fluent. I meet regularly with parents during the LiFT™ programme to sit down and discuss what is happening.

His mum smiled excitedly. 'He is so much better. I can't believe it after only one week of the LiFT™ programme.'

I replied, 'The changes are happening quickly because the LiFT™ is getting right to the cause of the problem – the ears' ability to work well together so that one ear can emerge as the lead ear.'

Week by week Nathaniel's fluency increased and became more established. When we began Phase Two of the LiFT™ programme we introduced the microphone, which further improved his fluency. I formally reviewed Nathaniel six weeks after the end of the LiFT™ programme and he was 100 per cent fluent. His mum saw the same excellent levels of fluency at home. We were excited as this had been the one area which had continued to pose problems – all the others were being resolved.

I reviewed Nathaniel twelve weeks later and again he was 100 per cent fluent. We were now in a position to work confidently in a direct manner on Nathaniel's speech sounds. Nathaniel's sounds are steadily improving and he has remained completely fluent.

In Nathaniel's case it became clear that his motor difficulties were impacting on his ability to be fluent. Of course this isn't true in all cases of dysfluency and that's why it is so important for speech and language therapists to develop an understanding of the body and how difficulties at the level of the body are reflected in the development of many skills, including speech and language skills.

Speech and language therapists need to look at 'the intelligence of the body,' as Leonardo Da Vinci did, to understand, firstly, why the child has speech and/or language difficulties and, secondly, how to develop the most effective treatment programmes. These programmes must include treating the body.

Paul Madaule's tripod analogy describes the intricate connections between the body – motor development – and the head – speech and language development. If the tripod is unsteady, how can you take a clear, focused picture or speak clearly. If the body is unsteady how can the head (mouth) produce words clearly and fluently. Some days you may be lucky but mostly you will find that it requires a steady tripod – a stable, developed and grounded body – to take a good picture or to speak clearly.

5

Sandy: the singer who didn't have a voice ....yet

Clinical diagnosis: specific language impairment and written language disorder

Sandy's GP originally referred him to me when he was three. He was one of a set of identical twins – and what delightful little guys they were. Both Sandy and Mark were referred for speech and language evaluations by their mum.

'It's Sandy I'm really worried about,' she explained. 'No one can understand him and his attention is all over the place compared to his twin.'

She didn't have any major concerns about Mark but she was worried about Sandy's poor attention and concentration and the fact that he couldn't follow simple instructions. I have worked with many sets of twins over the years and I'm always fascinated by how they communicate with each other and how they can be so connected. These guys were no different. They watched each other constantly. It was almost as if they were mirroring each other or trying to understand the world through their sibling's actions or reactions.

It was fascinating that they were so alike and at the same time so different. Mark was small and robust, with ginger hair and mischievous green eyes, whereas Sandy was tall and thin with a pale complexion and pale blue eyes. Mark loved to run, climb and play football and Sandy loved to sing. He could be engaged in an activity and the next thing he would break into song. His eyes would light up and off he would go. He could sing anything and had an interesting repertoire of songs. He didn't know all the words and he certainly didn't understand a lot of them but that didn't deter him in any way. He was a lovely singer but sometimes he could be off key and he didn't seem to be aware of it. This small fact gave me some important information about Sandy's ear-voice connection, that is the ability of his ear to monitor his own voice, speech, language and singing. Sandy had a poorly developed ear-voice connection, which was impacting on the development of his listening, speech and language development.

Formal assessment indicated that Mark had typically developing speech and language skills. However Sandy had a mild speech and language delay.

Sandy had a strong history of ear infections or 'glue ear' as it is often called, which predisposed him to having poor listening and attention skills, poor language comprehension, expression and speech production. A child may also experience difficulty with phonological awareness skills such as rhyming and segmenting, making these a challenge, and reading and reading comprehension. Sandy was also quite nasal and sounded hoarse. This masked his beautiful voice and at times seemed to discourage him from singing.

We made an immediate referral to a local ear, nose and throat consultant, to rule out any concerns about Sandy's vocal cords. We developed a comprehensive treatment programme for Sandy, which included standard speech and language techniques and a home programme of Therapeutic Listening®. Sandy's programme focused on developing his attention, listening and receptive language skills. Unfortunately, just as Sandy was due to begin his programme, his parents received word that the family was moving to another part of the country because of his dad's job. This meant that Sandy couldn't continue his speech therapy programme with me and I referred his family on to another speech and language therapist in their new location. His mum was to follow up his referral to his new therapist and the ear, nose and throat consultant.

I didn't hear a thing about Sandy until four years later, when he was eight. I had presumed that all was going well with him, until I received a call from his mum, to say they had moved back to the area and that she was concerned, even upset, about Sandy. His teachers had reported that he was inattentive in class, seemed to find it difficult to take in and retain information and his reading was more like that of a five and a half year old than an eight year old. We organised a review appointment as quickly as we could.

Both mum and dad attended the review with Sandy. It was funny to see him after the four years. He had hardly changed at all: he was just a taller, older version of the young Sandy I had known. His parents explained that he had followed an intensive speech and language therapy programme with an excellent therapist. Unfortunately the therapist was not trained in Therapeutic Listening® so Sandy had not had access to this element of the programme. His mum said: 'He has made some improvements but he is still unclear and the gap is widening between what he is able to do and what his friends are doing.'

The next step was to assess Sandy. During the assessment I noted that I had to tune in to decipher what he was saying. He had quite a rapid rate of speech – it was almost as if Sandy's brain was moving faster than his mouth. His mouth, or more specifically his tongue, lips and palate (the oral musculature that normally generates effective oral-motor movement), were not moving as quickly or as accurately and efficiently as they should have been. His articulators weren't moving as quickly as his brain and this was impacting on Sandy's overall intelligibility. His speech was quite unclear.

We then looked at Sandy's reading. His phonological awareness, which includes important pre-reading skills such as rhyming, were poor, as was his reading. As his mother had reported, at the age of eight he was achieving a reading age of five. However it was clear that there were other significant factors at play. Sandy's attention was limited and he was easily distracted. Many sounds seemed to distract him, both from inside and outside the assessment room, whether it was the sound of passing traffic or the heater coming on. He found it exceedingly difficult to come back to task once he was distracted and this was a real indicator of his level of listening and attention: he was not yet able to tune his listening in and out selectively. During the language assessment Sandy frequently looked at me in a puzzled fashion. This was particularly obvious on the comprehension test, where he was required to follow instructions of increasing length and complexity. He was experiencing difficulty processing the instructions auditorily.

Sandy's language profile was quite typical of a child who has a specific language impairment (SLI), the term used to describe any child who is not acquiring language in accordance with age-appropriate developmental patterns and known developmental sequences. I felt that if Sandy was struggling to understand what I was saying in this quiet clinic environment, it must have been tough for him to cope in the classroom and in the playground.

'It's a disaster,' his teacher told me on the phone. 'He can't listen. Everything distracts him, from the computer to the child in front of him. I don't know how he's learning at all.'

Just as I thought. Sandy was lost.

A surprising finding made by researchers at the University of California San Francisco, in 1997 provided evidence that SLI, which prevents so many children from keeping up in the classroom, is caused by an inability to process sound in the ear and is not, as previously thought, as a difficulty in higher brain regions. The discovery was originally reported in an article in the scientific journal *Nature*, which described how children with SLI fall behind in language skills in spite of having normal intelligence and apparently normal hearing. The difficulty relates to a reduced speed of processing of acoustic information. The source of the problem has been poorly understood and standard speech and language therapy has proved unsatisfactory in terms of helping children overcome the difficulty. When I worked in the public health system, I was encouraged to tell parents that SLI is a lifelong problem, that there would be some improvement with a lot of hard work but that the child wouldn't overcome their difficulties. The implications of this are vast in terms of the child and later the adult achieving their true potential both in learning and, more importantly, in life in general. We now know that children with SLI can overcome many of their difficulties by means of techniques that impact on the neuroplasticity of the brain, such as auditory interventions, particularly Therapeutic Listening® and the LiFT™ programmes.

Neuroscientist Dr Paula Tallal demonstrated that children with SLI (or LLI – Language Learning Impairment – as it is referred to in the US) require hundreds of milliseconds to discriminate between acoustic events, whilst children of the same age and intelligence levels who do not have the impairment require only tens of milliseconds to process the same sounds. They found that this basic sensory integration difficulty interferes with the ability of SLI (LLI) children to discriminate the critical brief acoustic cues within syllables and words that would enable them to distinguish one sound from another. This is a fundamental skill, not only when children are learning to understand language but when they are learning to read.

Doctors Tallal and Merzenich's neurophysiological studies of monkeys demonstrated that even in adult animals the neurons in the brain that map sensory events are highly 'plastic'. They found that the brain can reshape its neural circuitry in response to environmental experiences. They saw that the monkeys, by intensive training, could gradually improve their identification of faster and faster sounds. When they analysed the monkeys' brains they found that specialised auditory regions had reorganised and significantly expanded their neural circuits. They proposed that the training exercises used for the neural plasticity studies might be used to alleviate some of the sensory processing difficulties reported in SLI (LLI) children.

My experience has shown that auditory interventions such as Therapeutic Listening® and the LiFT™ programme impact significantly on the neuroplasticity of the brain. They work on the middle-ear, inner-ear and eighth cranial nerve connections into the brain stem and ultimately on each level of neural development. I regularly see children with SLI improving their language scores dramatically over the thirty-day LiFT™ programme – often by as much as two to three years. This is unheard of when traditional speech and language therapy techniques are used. This improvement means that the child is now able to approach speech, language and reading with a neural processing system more attuned to adequate online phonological processing, more like that of a child learning normally. That is what I wanted for Sandy and I knew it was achievable with the right intervention.

Looking at the pieces of Sandy's jigsaw we could see that there were four fundamental pieces. He had: a) a fast rate of speech; b) diminished voice quality; c) specific language impairment; and d) reading difficulties (written language disorder). From an assessment point of view I could see that there was a strong common thread here. All four areas of difficulty we identified can develop as a direct result of difficulty in the ear.

Quite simply a basic sensory integration difficulty in the ear can lead to difficulty filtering words, which impacts on the child's ability to identify the correct verbal information, something that is required for discrimination of sounds and words. This in turn is crucial for the effective and accurate understanding of language and development of phonological awareness for accurate reading. In short, the development of age-appropriate comprehension and reading skills are dependent on the effective integration of sensory information.

From a treatment perspective I wanted to identify an approach or combination of approaches that would have the biggest impact on Sandy, not just in one but all four areas of difficulty he was experiencing. Not only did I want him to achieve his potential, I wanted him to achieve it as quickly as possible. I knew the LiFT™ programme, combined with standard speech and language therapy, was the only option for Sandy as it would have an impact on most of the pieces of his jigsaw. It would improve Sandy's listening and attention skills. It would develop his ear-voice connection, so that he could monitor the rate, volume and clarity of his speech naturally and spontaneously. It would increase the speed and accuracy of his oral-motor movement, thereby improving the clarity of his speech. It would enhance his ability to filter important information and as a result his processing ability. It would develop the speed of his processing and comprehension and enhance his phonological awareness and reading ability. The LiFT™ programme, combined with speech and language therapy techniques, would have an impact on all levels of Sandy's neural development.

I began a thirty-day LiFT™ programme with Sandy. In the first fifteen days of the programme, the receptive phase, I could see the foundation stones being laid for the development of Sandy's attention, listening, comprehension and processing ability. His parents said that he was asking many more questions. On a number of occasions they had been surprised when he asked questions relating to their own conversations. His parents said: 'This would have gone completely over his head prior to the LiFT™.'

There was then an integration period of four weeks so that Sandy could assimilate and integrate what he had gained in the receptive phase. During this period Sandy also practised the reading out loud exercise (ROL) for ten minutes once a day. This a simple but highly effective technique that helps to develop the child's ear-voice connection or ear-voice loop. It encourages the child to use their right hand like a microphone in front of their mouth, which helps the low, middle and high frequencies to bounce back to the child's right ear, giving extra qualitative feedback.

Low frequency sounds are multidirectional and move quite a distance before they fade, making them easy for the ears to hear. However middle and high frequency sounds are unidirectional and tend to fade away quickly, often before they are picked up by the left and the right ears. These middle and high frequencies in our voices carry a great deal of qualitative information about our volume, rate, speed, resonance and clarity. In my experience many children with speech and language difficulties have a poorly developed ear-voice connection and this exacerbates their speech and language difficulties and extends their duration. The ROL exercise/microphone effect is a short-term measure to develop a child's ability to monitor the rate and volume of their own speech.

After the four-week integration period, Sandy started the second fifteen days of the programme – the expressive phase. Now I could see the pieces of Sandy's jigsaw falling into place. The expressive phase incorporates the microphone component for two half-hours a day and this has an impact on the child's ear-voice connection in the long term. I observed Sandy's rapid rate of speech reducing to a much more appropriate rate. He was becoming clear and intelligible and his receptive language skills were becoming firmly established at a more age-appropriate level. I could hear Sandy's reading accuracy and fluency improving day-by-day and I was looking forward to formally assessing his language skills six weeks after the end of the programme to see how far he had come. I could clearly see three out of four of the pieces of Sandy's jigsaw falling into place: the rate and clarity of his speech, his specific language impairment and his reading impairment.

However Sandy continued to experience a hoarseness that impacted on his voice quality (although not on its clarity). I referred Sandy back to his ear, nose and throat consultant and also on to a speech and language therapist colleague, who specialises in voice work with children. When I reviewed Sandy six months later and again one year later he was doing very well. His speech was crystal clear and there was no evidence of any specific language impairment. Sandy was understanding at an age-appropriate level and his language scores had improved by a dramatic three years over the period of a three-month programme. Sandy's reading ability and reading comprehension were now also age-appropriate. He was still not eager to read but was much better able to do it.

This didn't happen for Sandy alone but for most children I see who have SLI (LLI). These are the results that I expect from children with SLI who attend the LiFT™ programme. Some children with more significant difficulty or with more of a familial predisposition (hereditary component) may require a LiFT™ Boost or a number of LiFT™ Boosts to help them achieve their full language potential.

Having worked for a number of years in both junior and senior language units I know there are many children with SLI who are underachieving not only in the classroom but in life. It doesn't have to be like this. By using simple, non-invasive auditory intervention techniques such as Therapeutic Listening® and the LiFT™ programme, we can help these children overcome their language and learning difficulties and achieve their true ability in learning and in life.

6

Gabrielle: the socialite who didn't know how to talk...yet

Clinical diagnosis: verbal and motor dyspraxia

Gabrielle was a fascinating little lady, a real character, full of fun and mischief. But this wasn't at all the case when we first met. Gabrielle had been adopted from Russia at eight months old, by lovely parents who absolutely adored her. I still remember meeting Gabrielle for the first time. What an entrance she made. Her poor mum carried her into the assessment room, a thin little bundle, with straight brown hair and fiery eyes. She was crying her eyes out and clinging on to her mum for dear life. There were lots of tears and a little bit of looking at me from the corner of her eye. Gabrielle looked at me only long enough to work out where I was and that I was a safe distance away. She was determined to keep me and all strangers at arm's length.

Gabrielle was three when she came to see me, with a limited vocabulary of single words. She had approximately five words – 'hiya', 'mom', 'daddy', 'wee wee' and 'poo'. She was not able to string words together to make phrases. Her oral-motor imitation skills were non-existent, in that she couldn't copy any lip, tongue or palatal movements.

Gabrielle's comprehension was good but there was a big discrepancy between what she could understand and what she could say. From an articulation point of view she could sequence the sounds pretty well into the words she had. It was just that she had so few of them. She was quite non-verbal. I diagnosed a verbal dyspraxia with underlying sensory integration difficulties. A referral was also made to an occupational therapist trained in sensory integration, to ascertain whether there was a motor dyspraxia.

Verbal dyspraxia has been defined as 'difficulty with the control and coordination of learned patterns of movement, where there is no damage to muscles or nerves'. It may be present to varying degrees, from mild to severe. Most clinicians agree on the following diagnostic features and a child may exhibit one or more of these characteristics: a) difficulty in control of the speech apparatus; b) difficulty in speech sound production; c) difficulty sequencing sounds to make words; d) difficulty in regulating breathing and its speed, rhythm and volume; and e) difficulty sequencing words into phrases and sentences.

You are probably building up a picture of a little girl who couldn't communicate – but nothing could be further from the truth. In fact, given how little language Gabrielle had, it was hard to believe how well she communicated. There was nothing that she couldn't ask or tell her mum and dad. She used facial expressions, body-language, pointing, sounds – and if all that failed, she threw an almighty tantrum. I suppose this was part of the problem. She communicated brilliantly with her mum and dad but she wasn't interested in engaging with anyone else. It wasn't because she couldn't interact. She was quite proficient at that. However given her early history and sensory integration difficulties it was clear that she was experiencing attachment issues. She clung to her mum and dad week in, week out.

We tried the sessions in many different ways. Mum would come in and dad would stay out; dad would come in but mum would stay out; everyone would come in but I would stay out; mum and dad would come in and Gabrielle would stay out. She still didn't settle. It took time for Gabrielle to get to know me. Her mum said that this was how she typically engaged with adults other than herself and her husband. Usually children take to me pretty quickly as I do everything to ensure that they feel relaxed and at ease and are having fun. Not so with Gabrielle. She had been abandoned before and she wasn't going to be left again. She clung to her mum and watched my every move with frightened little eyes. There were no concerns about eye contact with Gabrielle: if anything she watched me too much. She was hyper-vigilant.

The information that was available about Gabrielle's early history was limited, which is often the case with children who have been adopted. However from observing her when she came to see me, it was possible to guess what her pre-adoptive history might have looked like: a) poor early stimulation; b) early sense of loss; c) poor sensory-motor development; d) either a familial predisposition to dyspraxia or possibly a premature birth, resulting in poor planning and sequencing ability, as these are thought to develop in the final four to six weeks of gestation; and e) a history of ear infections.

In my experience some or all of the above factors could have predisposed Gabrielle to her current challenges. No matter how early she was adopted, her history includes separation from her birth mother, the person who carried her for the first nine months of her life and is now gone. Some traumatic event during the pregnancy may also have influenced the way Gabrielle experienced the world.

Furthermore her mother's frame of mind and emotional status during the pregnancy may have influenced Gabrielle's experience of separation (Madaule, *Left Out: The Rejection Complex of the Adopted*, 1989). We know that the emotional status of the pregnant mother is transmitted to the unborn child in many ways, primarily through her voice. The ear is the first sensory organ to develop in the womb, allowing emotions such as apathy, anger and depression on the part of the mother to be perceived by the foetus. Psychologist Paul Madaule describes how these loaded messages influence the child's sense of being wanted or unwanted.

It was important to bear all this information in mind when developing a suitable treatment programme for Gabrielle. We needed a programme that would help Gabrielle to become calmer and more regulated and give her a better sense of herself, while at the same time improving her speech and language skills.

There were many pieces in Gabrielle's jigsaw that needed to be understood and treated effectively. We used Sensory Profile™, developed by Professor Winnie Dunn of the University of Kansas, who is well known in the field of sensory integration, to develop a better understanding of her sensory processing difficulties. This profile checklist was developed as a standard way for professionals to measure a child's sensory processing difficulties. The questionnaire consists of one hundred and twenty five items, grouped into three main categories, that look at how the senses process information.

When we applied this tool to Gabrielle it highlighted her difficulty processing vestibular, proprioceptive, tactile, oral and auditory sensory information. Many sections of her profile fell outside the typical performance range, highlighting her difficulties in specific areas. In line with the theory I had formulated about Gabrielle's sensory processing difficulties, I could see that she was experiencing more difficulty with touch processing than with movement processing. She also displayed poor oral sensory processing. But it was Gabrielle's difficulty in processing specific sound frequencies that was her greatest challenge: she had a significant auditory defensiveness.

Auditory defensiveness has been described as an over-sensitivity to certain sounds or sound frequencies. It can result in a fight or flight reaction as the child tries to cope with specific sounds, or children may make excessive amounts of noise to block out the offensive sounds. Auditory defensiveness can relate to very low frequency sounds – sounds below 300 hertz that carry limited, if any spatial information. Children with poor ability to process spatial information have real difficulty with these sounds and can react negatively to them. Sounds that fit within this category are hair dryers, hand dryers, vacuum cleaners, food mixers, computers and the hum of fluorescent lights. Children with this kind of auditory defensiveness find it difficult to localise the sound and work out where it is coming from.

Auditory defensiveness also relates to loud, unpredictable sounds, such as motorbikes, lawn mowers and thunder. Sheila Frick explains that the middle-ear muscles have a two-fold neuromuscular role. The first is to prevent sensory overload and the second is to enhance sound discrimination. Sound reduction is accomplished by reflex contraction and relaxation of these middle-ear muscles, which take place about one-eighth of a second after one or both ears is exposed to a loud external sound. These muscles also protect the inner ear from fatigue and prevent sensory overload in the nervous system. Last but certainly not least, they contract to protect the individual from self-generated internal sounds. For example, they contract just before a person vocalises to protect the nervous system from the intensity of one's own voice.

In 1989 Counter and Borg did some interesting research into the role of the ear. They found that the middle ear muscles contract within one second of being presented with a loud sound. Within one eighth of a second of hearing a passing train at its loudest, the middle ear 'zooms out' and therefore no longer hears the noise at the same intensity. This protects the inner ear and central nervous system from sensory overload.

Gabrielle had difficulty both with low frequency sounds and with loud, unpredictable sounds. For example she couldn't bear to hear the toilet flushing or to use hand dryers in public toilets. The hair dryer and the vacuum cleaner drove her so crazy that she would run out of the room with her hands over her ears. She would scream at the sound of thunder and lawn mowers were a complete no no.

We needed to help Gabrielle to overcome her sensory processing difficulties and in particular her auditory defensiveness, as it was causing her such distress and anxiety. A sensory diet, which is a programme of sensory activities, was developed specifically for her, in order to deal with her sensory processing challenges. An integral component of this was a Therapeutic Listening® programme and a little later a LiFT™ programme. This sensory diet enabled Gabrielle to process sensory information much more effectively, resulting in a one hundred per cent improvement in her auditory defensiveness. We also observed significant improvements in Gabrielle's oral and general sensory processing. The sensory diet had an impact on many other areas, including attention/listening, comprehension, auditory processing, spatial awareness, regulation, expressive language, interaction and engagement and social skills.

Interestingly, although auditory defensiveness often presents itself as a severe difficulty, it can easily be resolved. In fact I've yet to see a child whose auditory defensiveness I couldn't resolve. In my experience auditory intervention is the key, in particular Therapeutic Listening® and the LiFT™ programme.

The first piece of the jigsaw had fallen into place. Now it was time to consider another important piece of Gabrielle's jigsaw – her over-attachment to her adoptive parents and lack of attachment to others.

'She won't let us out of her sight,' her dad explained in exasperation. 'She just gets so upset. How is she going to go to school?'

Thankfully school wasn't in Gabrielle's immediate future but there was no doubt that we needed to look at how to help Gabrielle develop a relaxed attachment to her new family, by making the bond between the adoptive mother and Gabrielle a more natural one.

By using the LiFT™, we could incorporate Gabrielle's adoptive mum's voice into her programme. We have used this technique with many families and it has proved highly successful. A recording of the adoptive mum's voice is made at a recording studio. The recording is then intensified, particularly in the high frequency range, to emulate what the child would have heard within the womb. The recordings require the adoptive mum to talk to her adopted child, welcoming him or her to the family, saying how much they have been looking forward to them arriving and becoming part of their family. The mum also sings rhymes, songs and lullabies and possibly reads to the child. I've watched many mums being recorded and its one of the most moving things I've ever witnessed.

Using the LiFT™ helped to make the bond between Gabrielle and her mum a more natural and positive one. Week-by-week she became less intense and much more relaxed and spontaneous about her engagement with her mum and dad and with everyone else. It was a pleasure to watch her.

'We can actually go out for a night together and get a babysitter in,' her dad explained proudly.

We had brought together two crucial pieces of Gabrielle's jigsaw and laid the foundations for the development of her higher-level skills, including regulation, listening, comprehension, expressive ability and social skills.

Gabrielle attended speech and language therapy with me for two years. We combined sound therapy with speech and language therapy techniques to help Gabrielle achieve her full potential. Incorporating the LiFT™ programme allowed us to tackle areas that we would not have been able to touch up to then.

Using the LiFT™ programme and incorporating her adoptive mum's voice helped Gabrielle to became more relaxed and regulated in her attachment to her beautiful mum and dad. She engaged much more eagerly with others, to the point that I started to call her 'the hostess with the mostest'. In fact Gabrielle became so engaging that when one day during her LiFT™ Boost programme the doorbell rang, I went to see who was there, only to find that Gabrielle had got there before me to welcome our guests. This happened on many occasions. The little girl who was originally not interested in engaging with anyone was now willing to talk to everyone.

7

All the little people who haven't achieved their potential...yet

Children with sensory defensiveness

Why does he grind his teeth, why does she touch everything, why will he not touch anything; why does he rub himself on the floor; why does she flap; why does he rock; why does she spin; why does he jump up and down; why does she bite her shirt; why did he bite the dog... why? bewildered parents ask.

I use the word 'bewildered' intentionally, as at first the behaviour of the child may seem strange, unusual, even frightening. Parents naturally wonder if this behaviour means that their child has more severe difficulties than originally thought? Will he always do this? Does this make her stand out more from other children? The answer to all these questions is no. If we looked at the world through the eyes of a child, we would see exactly what they are doing and why. The 'strange' behaviour that they seem to crave is in reality straightforward, natural and obvious – if only we looked at the world through the eyes of a child.

At this point I don't think there is any behaviour that I haven't seen and none of these behaviours surprise me, because in every case the behaviour has started as a response to a particular sensory input. The child likes it, then the child starts to seek it. This behaviour is giving the child some sensory feedback that they like. If we can look at the world through the eyes of a child and see what this feedback is, we can feed the sense in question in a more productive manner. This will result in a more regulated child who no longer seeks that 'strange behaviour'. I believe that most behaviours in children have a sensory basis or foundation. If we can establish what this is we can learn how to remediate it through a sensory diet.

The term 'sensory diet' was coined by two occupational therapists, Patricia and Julia Wilbarger, to describe a programme treating sensory defensiveness (a child's tendency to react negatively to specific sensory input generally considered harmless). The concept of a sensory diet is that the individual requires a certain amount of activity and sensation to be at their most alert, adaptable and skilful. This is much like a person's nutritional requirements but in this instance we are feeding their senses with specific nutritious activities. These activities often span a number of senses and can include any or all the following: vestibular, proprioceptive, auditory, tactile, oral and visual. The sensory diet is tailor made to meet the sensory needs of the child and its primary aim is to help those with sensory defensiveness feel calm, alert and organised most of the time by using special activities that are scheduled throughout the day.

In *Sensory Defensiveness in Children Aged 2-12: An Intervention Guide for Parents and Other Caretakers* (1991), the Wilbargers describe how 'each person with sensory defensiveness develops his or her own set of behaviours, which are usually a combination of sensory avoiding and sensory seeking behaviours'. Different types of sensory defensiveness can be attributed to each of the sensory systems. For example children who are tactile defensive tend to avoid touch, perceiving it as negative, harmful and even painful. They tend to dislike being touched, preferring to instigate touch, ensuring that it is on their own terms. As infants they often dislike touch experiences such as bathing, feeding and nappy changing.

'And don't talk to me about preschool. It was a complete disaster,' Harry's dad exclaimed. 'Of course we didn't realise it at the time but all that tactile input through the sand play, water play, playing with paints and play dough nearly drove him crazy.'

As older children the tactile defensive are often irritated by certain types of clothing, care labels or new clothes. They may dislike being close to others and avoid crowds. They may hate having their hands and face dirty. Some may bump and crash into things as a way of seeking deep-pressure touch. Children who are tactile defensive tend to dislike light touch in particular, preferring a deeper, firmer touch.

On the other hand children who are orally defensive tend to dislike or avoid certain food textures and types of food.

'She is such a picky eater,' Ellie's mum explained guiltily. 'She will eat only soft, bland foods. I don't know what to do with her and I feel so guilty about it.' This is typical of what parents say to me all the time about their children's eating habits.

Gravitational insecurity is another form of sensory defensiveness, this time relating to movement. Children with gravitational insecurity often have an 'irrational fear of change in position or movement'(Wilbarger). These children may have an intense fear of their feet leaving the ground or having their head tipped backwards.

As one mum explained about her son: 'I think all his difficulties started when we used to wash his hair in the sink. We used to tip his head back, even though it really upset him. He became so nervous and anxious after that and he still mentions it even now, years later.'

Postural insecurity means that children are fearful of certain types of movement activities. This is often quite a realistic fear as it reflects the child's poor postural control or mechanisms.

Children who are visually defensive may be oversensitive to light and can be quite distractible visually. These children may avert their eyes or seem to avoid eye contact.

Auditory defensiveness refers to an over-sensitivity to specific sounds or frequencies of sound. Other sensitivities can develop in relation to taste and/or smell.

Most of the children I see have sensory issues, which are at the very least contributing to and quite possibly causing their communication difficulties. In fact it is quite rare that I see a child with communication difficulties who doesn't have an underlying sensory defensiveness component. For example we all know of a child who seeks movement, to the point that it interferes with their ability to sit, listen and concentrate. This is the child who may have difficulty understanding and using language. Or the child who is orally defensive, who is possibly a 'picky eater' who dislikes having his teeth brushed. This child often presents with articulation difficulties as he dislikes the sensation of light touch in his mouth. When we speak we move our tongues lightly against various articulators within the oral area, for example, the palate, the teeth and the lips. So if the child dislikes light touch in the oral area he will be less inclined to want to speak and in my experience often tries to avoid certain sounds that involve this light sensation, particularly the alveolar sounds – for example [t], [d] and velar sounds such as [k] and [g].

Another example is the child with a tactile defensiveness, who avoids certain touch sensations. This child will often stand back and observe, rather than get involved in engaging with his peers. This can lead to diminished ability to interact and engage, resulting in limited social skills.

There are many other examples and it is children with various kinds of sensory defensiveness who ultimately present in speech and language therapy clinics all over the world with speech, language and communication challenges. I have worked all over the world and have collected many stories of children with sensory defensiveness along the way that I would like to share with you to reassure you that when you look at the world through the eyes of your child, everything makes sense.

I was fortunate to have had the opportunity to live and work in New Zealand a number of years ago. I worked in group special education, with the best and most dedicated of teachers and therapists. As part of my job I travelled from school to school, working with children with communication difficulties. The children were all fascinating but a few stand out in my mind. Ariel was one such child. He was a gorgeous little guy, with a really cheeky smile, twinkling eyes and the curliest black hair.

Ariel, who was five and had just started school, had cerebral palsy. When I first met him I could see that Ariel was a busy little guy who needed to be on the move all the time. In fact he gave the impression that if he didn't keep moving he would fall down. He didn't appear to have the core stability required to keep him on the ground in a standing position; hence all the additional movement. I could also see that he was having real difficulty attending and listening. He seemed to be a little lost in space, not quite sure where he was. His teacher said that his attention, listening and comprehension skills were all reasons for concern.

'I know it sounds strange,' his teacher reported to me, 'but Ariel's greatest difficulty is his response to the toilet flushing.'

I know this may seem like a little thing but it was a big issue for Ariel. It was causing him deep upset to the point that he wouldn't go to the toilet at school. This was a problem as he was in school from nine in the morning until three in the afternoon. He needed to go to the toilet at least twice during his school day and he was terrified of using the school toilet.

Where would you begin to treat something like this? Firstly we had to identify the frequency band of the offensive sound. Yes, by listening to the toilet flushing. We didn't want to subject Ariel to this sound unnecessarily but at the same time we needed to see how he responded. He became hysterical once the toilet began to flush. He was terrified, looking all around, almost searching for the sound. He couldn't localise the sound to the toilet cistern. What was happening? Toilet flushing is a low frequency sound that is below 300 herz, which means that it carries limited spatial information. Children who find this sound particularly difficult to cope with tend to have poor spatial awareness, so such sounds can be overwhelming and frightening.

We developed a sensory diet for Ariel, an important component of which was his Therapeutic Listening® programme. In addition I liaised with his physiotherapist and occupational therapist in developing a suitable programme of heavy work activities to help to regulate his nervous system. (Heavy work or proprioceptive input is the performance of tasks that involves heavy resistance and input to the muscles and joints. These can comprise oral, whole body or hand activities.)

Ariel's Therapeutic Listening® programme began with the 'Ease #1' CD, which he listened to twice a day for two weeks. This is a disc from the Therapeutic Listening® range which helps to activate the middle ear muscles so that he could begin to process sounds correctly. We then blended in the 'Sounds of Nature' CD for fifteen minutes once a day. This is an interesting CD, which works on developing an individual's spatial awareness by giving him his own reference point in space, like giving a person the red dot in the shopping mall life so that he knows where he is. It then becomes much easier to work out where other people are and where sounds are coming from. Ariel's auditory defensiveness gradually decreased and was completely resolved in four weeks.

I continued with his Therapeutic Listening® programme for a further two months to ensure that the auditory defensiveness was well and truly gone. Ariel was still scared to go to the school toilet, as he didn't know that he could now cope with the offensive sound. His psychologist, his classroom assistant and I developed a behavioural type programme to help to desensitise Ariel and he gradually realised that the toilet was safe and that the sound of the toilet flushing didn't bother him any longer. Now going to the toilet has become a pleasure for Ariel and not the torture that it previously was.

After this I'd say I developed a bit of a reputation as a sound girl so it was no surprise that everyone turned to me when a call came into the clinic about a girl of eight with auditory issues. Her name was Muriel. She was from the Pacific Islands, attending school locally in Auckland, and had a developmental delay. Interestingly her teacher's greatest concern was not how to optimise her language and learning abilities as she felt they had these under control. Instead her concern was Muriel's response to thunder. She was so frightened that she became almost hysterical when there was thunder. It was winter in Auckland and although the weather can be beautiful at that time of year, it can also be quite unpredictable, with four seasons in a day. So there could be thunder at any time. I met Muriel, a beautiful young girl. Her family had moved to New Zealand a number of years earlier in search of a better life. She had long, curly black hair that almost reached her waist and the most frightened green eyes I had ever seen. She looked around anxiously, almost waiting for the offensive sound to manifest.

Looking at what was happening with Muriel's body I could see straight away that she had low muscle tone. Her teacher confirmed that her coordination was poor, so this predisposed her to having low muscle tone not only in the body but also in the middle ear. This brings us back to the way Counter and Borg (1989) described the passing train and how within one eighth of a second the ear should 'zoom out' or pull away from the noise. What was happening to Muriel was similar to the noise of the passing train but her ear was not zooming out so she was hearing the sound of the thunder at its most intense for a much longer period than she should do and this was overwhelming her nervous system. Her middle ear muscles, more specifically the stapedius reflex, was not working effectively.

We introduced a Therapeutic Listening® programme of 'Ease #1' and 'Baroque' for modulation, to reactivate the middle ear muscles and encourage them to move more quickly and effectively. This programme was carried out twice a day at school. Within two weeks of the beginning of the programme, her teacher came running down the hall to meet me. She told me that Muriel was responding in a much more appropriate manner to the sound of thunder, something she found incredible after such a short time. She could see that it didn't frighten her the way it had before. We continued Muriel's Therapeutic Listening® programme for six weeks longer to ensure that she was calmer, much more regulated and listening better.

I remember too a little guy called Donel whom I saw in Dublin, a busy boy of three who moved constantly. He jumped up and down, twirled and flapped regularly during the assessment. His mother was worried sick and Donel had already been seen by child psychiatry services when I met him. They hadn't made an official diagnosis but had mentioned a possible diagnosis of PDD-NOS (pervasive developmental delay, not otherwise specified). This is one of five forms of autistic spectrum disorder. Because it is a spectrum disorder not every child will show the same signs but there are characteristically two main areas of difficulty: social interaction skills and communication.

Donel certainly had significant language issues and quite a scattered profile of ability. There were lots of inconsistencies, which is a good sign, as it means there is movement, there are changes. We needed to look at Donel's ceiling of ability across a number of areas and also look at his baseline skills. With the right techniques I know we should be able to achieve the ceiling levels much more of the time. Donel was a fun little guy. He was distracted, finding it difficult to work out where he was in time and space. He had that woozy look in his eyes, which is so typical of children who are lost in space. His body was busy looking for opportunities for movement: that is vestibular input. No wonder he was finding it so difficult to attend, listen or engage. If we could give him a better sense of himself in time and space, I wondered if he would 'land' and as a result be better able to listen, attend and understand.

We started Donel on a LiFT™ programme, incorporating lots of heavy work (proprioceptive) activities. Within two weeks of starting the programme I could see Donel 'landing'. He didn't need to jump up and down or spin himself any longer. His movement/vestibular system was starting to process movement information more effectively and as a result he no longer needed non-productive movement. By the end of the third week his mum said he had stopped flapping. There are numerous reasons why children flap. In Donel's case he was flapping because his vestibular system was becoming overwhelmed and he was trying to calm himself.

An integration period of four weeks followed and then we began phase two, during which Donel firmly established his listening and language skills. I reviewed Donel eight weeks after the end of the programme. His mum was thrilled. He no longer flapped or jumped or twirled himself. He was grounded. He was listening. He was engaging. His language skills had improved significantly. Donel is scheduled to do a LiFT™ Boost programme to develop his skills even further.

So many children I see are lost in time and space. They have such poorly developed temperospatial reasoning that they are not sure where they are or how they got there. Once they get a better sense of time and space through the music, the pieces of their developmental jigsaw begin to come together much better. I remember three little boys coming in to see me one after the other one day. I'm a little superstitious about events happening in threes: I always feel there must be something important to learn so I sit up and take notice. I have found over the years that children with similar difficulties come to me in clusters, as if to teach me how to help them in the most effective way. Certain children get lost in the bigger space – the classroom, the yard, the playground and big treatment rooms. I thought I was great with my big treatment room; little did I know that I would have been better off working in a box.

One after the other, the little guys entered the big treatment space. Like Theo, whom I described in Chapter 2, they got lost, ping-ponging from one activity to the other and becoming more and more overwhelmed until they found the box. The cardboard box that was sitting in the corner became the most important, most valuable room in the centre that day. One by one those three little guys climbed into the empty cardboard box. The ping-ponging stopped. The calmness returned. The boys became more engaged and noticeably more connected. Initially the boys were like liquids flowing into the big room, the big space. They had no boundaries. They would flow into any space they happened to be in. The larger the space, the more they would flow into it.

The opposite was also true. The smaller the space, the less the boys could flow and the more they felt they had boundaries. At last they knew where their arms were, where their legs were and most importantly where they were in space. That cardboard box, that small container, gave them the sense of something great. It gave them the end points, the boundaries that they couldn't find in their own body. It gave them the sense of where their body ended and the rest of the world began.

The cardboard box gave me an important piece of information about why the boys were finding it so difficult to make eye contact, to listen, to interact and engage. We introduced each of the boys to a programme of Therapeutic Listening®, initially using Mozart, then 'Ease', combined with the 'Sounds of Nature' CD. The boys began to develop an understanding of space and where they were in space through the music. The building blocks of space and time were being laid, with excellent results. Each of the boys began to look, listen and connect more. The fundamental pieces of their jigsaws were beginning to come together and we built on them, block by block.

I'm often referred children who tend to 'mouth' non-food items, for example toys and clothes. I've also seen children who mouth or lick paint, furniture, and metal pipes. The reason is always the same. The oral area – the mouth – contains a high concentration of tactile receptors in a very small area. Often children who seek more information through the mouth, by exploring objects orally, are not processing tactile information correctly. They try to compensate by 'mouthing' objects.

Of course there is a stage in a child's development when mouthing is totally normal and natural. It is the child's way of exploring the world and is to be expected for their age. I am talking about children who continue to use their mouths to explore for a more extended period.

Dina was one such child. I met him originally at the Listening Therapy Centre in Galway, when he had just turned four. He was cute, with blonde spiked hair and a cheeky little face, but it isn't his appearance that sticks in my memory as much as the way he behaved. He was like a tornado. I can safely say the assessment room has never been the same. He took the room apart: every shelf was cleared, every box emptied and every toy mouthed. He was originally referred with a diagnosis of developmental delay, meaning that each area of his development was supposedly delayed – his language, his coordination, his play, his interaction, everything.

When Dina was assessed, however, it became clear that his language processing and expressive ability were much more typical of a child with a specific language impairment – that is more a disordered than a delayed profile, which indicates areas of real ability. True, he wasn't understanding or processing language the way he should have been and he certainly found it difficult to express himself. However I could see that with the right interventions, he had the ability to progress much further. His play was quite typical for his age, plenty of symbolic, pretend play with Spiderman and Batman. However he mouthed toys constantly during the assessment. It was obvious that this need to mouth objects was distracting him from engaging in more appropriate play, language and interaction.

His mum was concerned about this. A variety of professionals had highlighted to her on many occasions that this was a strong indicator of Dina's developmental stage and of his overall ability. I didn't agree at all. My theory was that Dina was mouthing, not because this was the level he was functioning at cognitively, like a much younger child, but because he had underlying sensory processing difficulties. If I was correct, a sensory approach was the key to helping Dina overcome his difficulties.

We immediately introduced a sensory diet, which comprised of a Therapeutic Listening® programme, an oral massage programme and the Wilbarger Touch Brushing Protocol. I reviewed Dina four weeks later and his mum was excited. Dina was starting to improve. Not only had his mouthing decreased significantly, he was understanding language better. We continued to develop Dina's Therapeutic Listening® programme over the following six months, so that we could help him be more regulated and move through the correct developmental stages. Dina is progressing nicely. He no longer mouths objects. His language skills are age appropriate and he attends mainstream school without any additional help.

Dina's story demonstrates how important it is for people assessing children to understand how poor sensory processing and sensory integrative difficulties can have a negative impact on each level of neural development. These sensory issues can easily be worked on to improve a child's speech and language development. By incorporating simple sensory techniques we can help children to listen better, be calmer and more focused and ultimately better able to master speech and language skills.

Magical things will happen when listening comes alive. It will inspire you with hope because in the words of Andy Dufresne in *The Shawshank Redemption*: 'Hope is a good thing, maybe the best of things.'

There is hope that your child can reach his educational

potential; hope that your child can reach his language potential; hope that your child can reach his learning potential and, most importantly of all, hope that your child can reach his life potential, at last sharing his own unique gift with the world.

8

What you can do for your child

In 2008 I created a DVD programme for parents called: *Speech and Language Therapy for your Child: A New Way of Learning and Thinking*. In it I describe to parents firstly how to assess and secondly how to begin to treat their child's sensory needs. This will help parents to identify sensory issues that their child may be experiencing so that they can develop a sensory diet to help their child to be more regulated and calmer, to listen better and to be more open to engagement. This chapter contains the same information.

Firstly you need to observe your child to see if they are seeking or avoiding certain sensory stimuli. By using the sensory checklist below you can decide whether your child has some sensory issues and then work out exactly which sensory inputs your child is seeking and avoiding.. Please tick the statements that you feel are appropriate to your child.

Sensory Checklist

Auditory

Avoiding

a) Is startled or distressed by loud noises ☐

b) Covers ears with hands for certain sounds/noises ☐

c) Dislikes certain low frequency sounds, for example hair dryer, hand dryer, food-mixer ☐

Seeking

d) Finds it difficult to work with background noise ☐
e) Appears not to hear what you say ☐
f) Has difficulty paying attention ☐
g) Has difficulty following instructions ☐

Touch

Avoiding

a) Regularly becomes upset during grooming, for example, washing, hair brushing ☐
b) Can over-react to touch ☐
c) Resists cuddling, pulls away from touch ☐

Seeking

d) Enjoys crashing and bumping into objects and people ☐
e) Constantly touches people and objects ☐
f) Seems unaware of face and hands being messy ☐

Movement

Avoiding

a) Can become anxious when moving or when experiencing movement ☐
b) Fears falling and heights ☐
c) Becomes upset or sick when travelling in the car ☐

Seeking

d) Constantly moving or running about ☐
e) Moves so much that it interferes with other activities ☐
f) Finds it difficult to concentrate because of the need to move ☐

Taste

Avoiding

a) Avoids certain food tastes or textures ☐
b) Dislikes brushing teeth ☐
c) Could be described as a picky eater ☐

Seeking

d) Enjoys foods that you wouldn't expect, for example, sour, bitter, spicy ☐
e) Likes to chew on non-food items ☐
f) Is unaware of food or liquid on his face ☐

Body

a) Becomes tired easily ☐
b) Has poor endurance ☐
c) Has a weak grasp ☐
d) Seeks lots of rough and tumble play ☐
e) Poor articulation ☐

Children react differently to various kinds of sensory input. For example the child who seeks lots of movement (vestibular seeking), may avoid touch (tactile avoiding) or may have no difficulty at all with touch. Therapists are always looking for the extremes in response to sensory stimuli – that is the child either seeking or avoiding the sensory input. By now you will have identified what your child is seeking and avoiding and what senses are most affected: for example the body, movement, taste, auditory, touch or vision.

Below is a comprehensive list of activities that can be used with your child to help him to be calmer, more focused and more regulated. You can create your own tailor-made home programme for your child. For example if your child is avoiding touch activities look to the touch-avoiding section for activities to develop your child's sense of touch. If your child is seeking movement activities, look to the movement-seeking section to find activities to help your child become calmer and more focused.

Movement sense activities

These will help your child to concentrate and focus and are suitable for children of three years and over.

If your child is seeking lots of movement activities encourage him to:

- swing on a swing set (with support if required)
- use a space-hopper, sit'n'spin, trampoline (under supervision)

If your child avoids movement activities/experiences he will benefit from:

- sliding with assistance
- swinging gently in a back and forth action with assistance with lots of deep-pressure hugs

Touch sense activities

These will help your child to be less fidgety, calmer and more focused. Children who avoid touch tend to perceive it as negative, harmful, even painful.

If your child avoids touch experiences do the following:

- firm, predictable touch is favourable
- deep-pressure massage on the skin
- after bath time, use deep-pressure massage to towel dry.
- when cutting nails, provide deep-pressure on the tip of each finger prior to cutting the nail. The same technique can be used when washing or brushing hair.

Children who seek lots of touch are often not perceiving it accurately and therefore crave touch to get more information.

If your child seeks lots of touch do the following:

- play with clay, sand, finger-paints and play dough: provide lots of different tactile experiences.
- hide objects in bags of rice and have the child try to find object without looking.
- sandwich between two cushions or children (always ensure that your child's head is clear).

Sense of taste (mouth)

If you find that you child is reluctant to put things in his mouth or is a picky feeder try the following:

- do deep-pressure massage with your finger on the lips, tongue and palate.
- give opportunities to try lots of different foods.
- offer fun sucking and blowing activities, for example, blowing bubbles, balloons, respiratory toys.

Taste sense (mouth) activities will also prepare your child for speech and language work so you could:

- use an electric toothbrush firmly on the tongue and the roof of the mouth.
- encourage a variety of food textures and tastes, for example, lemon, peppermint, salty and spicy foods.

Body activities

All children enjoy and benefit from body activities, so it is a good idea to incorporate some body activities into your sensory programme. These are calming and organising, as information from your muscles and joints helps to organise your nervous system.

Some examples of body activities are:

- playing push and pull games
- digging in sand and carrying buckets of sand
- bouncing on a hippety-hoppety ball
- helping you to carry in groceries, take rubbish out, do the vacuuming

At school your child can do body activities by becoming teacher's helper.

My experience over the past seventeen years has shown that Therapeutic Listening® and the LiFT™ programme are fundamental components of any sensory diet as they help to regulate the senses at the level of the brain stem. In my experience, it is important that the sensory programme is implemented at least two weeks prior to the introduction of the speech and language programme. This is to lay firm foundations so that the speech and language techniques used will be even more effective. When your child is calmer and more focused he will be much more ready to learn new speech and language skills. The sensory programme should continue for at least two months – and often much longer – to help your child to remain calm, focused and learning language.

At this point your child's sensory behaviours should have reduced significantly and in most cases should have disappeared altogether. The sensory reason for the child to seek the behaviour no longer exists, although I have noted that a small percentage of children may persist in seeking the behaviour. Once the original sensory reason for the behaviour has been removed, a habit factor may at times persist. In this instance it is important to introduce a simple behaviour-type programme to break the habit. A variety of programmes is available, including token and other simple reward systems. You will soon see that these 'strange' behaviours that you were so concerned about aren't that strange at all. They aren't specific to your child. They aren't even specific to your country. They are simply ways that children learn to regulate their own nervous systems, to help them to feel at ease in the world.

If we look at the world through the eyes of a child we will learn to see what children see and understand what they do and why they do it.

9

Sound therapy programmes

A growing number of speech and language therapists incorporate sound-based technologies into their work. These programmes combine the therapeutic benefits of music with sophisticated sound technology. Auditory and sound-based interventions require the client to listen to recordings that have been designed to produce specific effects on listening skills as part of a prescribed programme. All programmes require detailed assessment to be undertaken by a qualified clinician. There are many music and sound therapy programmes available today, which can make it confusing for parents who would like to incorporate an auditory intervention into their child's therapy programme. Here is a short description of the best known and most popular sound therapy programmes utilised by experienced health and educational professionals worldwide.

The Tomatis Method (www.tomatis.com)

This was created in the mid-1950s by Dr Alfred Tomatis, a French ear, nose and throat specialist. Tomatis is considered to be the founder of sound therapy and it is fair to say that most of the therapeutic auditory interventions are based on his early work. Tomatis originally described the role of the ear as the 'integrator', providing organisation at all levels of the nervous system. He made the connection between the development of a child's ability to listen and their development of receptive, expressive language, their motivation to pay attention and the refinement of their motor control. The Tomatis Method defines listening as 'the ability to use one's hearing intentionally and attentively, and in a way that is acceptable on an emotional level, for the purpose of learning and communicating'.

Hearing is passive but listening is dynamic and requires an action: its implementation implies the ability to select an acoustic message among others, to inhibit sounds which are not relevant, to constantly readjust the content and the form of this message, and to immediately evaluate the result of this control' (www.tomatis.com). Any distortions in the ability to listen properly can lead to difficulties in every aspect of daily life. The Tomatis Method seeks to determine the causes of any listening difficulties or distortions and to regulate them.

The therapeutic tool used in this clinic-based programme is called the Electronic Ear. This system electronically imitates the brain's natural ability to organise and manage sound. In doing so it aims to restore the proper function of the auditory muscles in the inner ear. Once properly functioning, these muscles will enable the client to inhibit or select sounds correctly in their environment, according to their relevance.

During the treatment programme, each child listens to classical music such as Mozart or Gregorian chant and in some cases their mother's voice over headphones. There are two phases of treatment: a receptive and an expressive phase. The programme takes place over a forty-five day period, which is split into a fifteen-day course followed by three separate periods of ten days. It takes place under the expertise of a practitioner trained in the Tomatis Method.

The LiFT™ or Listening Fitness Programme
(www.listeningfitness.com; www.listeningcentre.com)
Canadian psychologist Paul Madaule developed this intensive listening programme in 1999. Madaule was originally a client and colleague of Dr Tomatis in France and he became his close confidante: together they opened the first Listening

Centre in Toronto. Madaule writes extensively about listening skills, difficulties and treatment in his book *When Listening Comes Alive*, which I would recommend to anyone looking for a comprehensive explanation of this subject. The LiFT™ programme takes place in-clinic but can also take place at home, if this is recommended by the practitioner. The programme is called after the small, mobile piece of equipment known as the LiFT™ (Listening Fitness Trainer), which is used progressively to filter sound frequencies in Mozart's music, Gregorian chant and sometimes the mother's voice. The mobility and flexibility of the equipment facilitate the child's movement, exploration and interaction. The programme also includes two phases: the receptive or passive phase that finely tunes listening skills and 'opens up the ear', and the expressive phase or active phase which involves a lot of microphone work. Through talking, singing, reading and humming, the client improves expressive ability, including speech, reading, language, movement, voice and confidence. The programme usually takes place over a thirty-day period, which is split into two fifteen-day phases, separated by an integration period of between two and six weeks. This programme also takes place under the expert supervision of a qualified practitioner.

AIT – Auditory Integration Training (www.aithelps.com)

Developed by another French colleague of Tomatis, Dr Guy Berard, this programme incorporates many of the Tomatis techniques by refining the filtering equipment used to deliver the programme. 'The Berard Auditory Integration Training was designed to normalise hearing and the ways in which the brain processes auditory information' (www.aithelps.com). A bespoke programme is designed for clients, according to their sensitivities to sound frequencies. If a client is hypersensitive to frequencies of 1000 and 8000 hertz, for example, they will become over-stimulated or disoriented when exposed to these frequencies. The AIT method works at normalising the client's response across all frequencies within normal range of human hearing. The client will listen to specifically chosen lively music, with a broad range of frequencies, for two and a half hours per day with a total of ten hours completed over twelve days. The programme can be used within a clinic or school setting under the supervision of an AIT practitioner.

Therapeutic Listening® (www.vitallinks.net)
Developed by Sheila Frick, an eminent American occupational therapist, Therapeutic Listening® is an auditory intervention programme that uses the organised sound patterns inherent in music to impact on all levels of the nervous system. Frick, emphasises the importance of using sound in combination with sensory integrative treatment techniques to promote and support the emergence of many fundamental skills. The programme provides the client with a number of electronically altered recordings within a tailored sensory integrative framework. Therapeutic Listening® can take place at home, at school or in the clinic but must also be developed and supervised by a trained therapist.

Samonas Sound Therapy (www.samonas.com)
Again building on the groundbreaking work of Tomatis, this programme was developed by Ingo Steinbach in Germany. Steinbach, an acoustic physicist, developed his programme based on the laws of physics as they relate to sound, combined with the established principles of music therapy. The Samonas programme uses specific headphones and recordings in the provision of the programme over a period of weeks, months or even years, depending on the needs of the client. The programme can take place at home, in school or in-clinic but must be developed and supervised by a trained professional.

At the Listening Therapy Centre in Galway, we use three forms of sound therapy: Therapeutic Listening® (including Advanced Therapeutic Listening®), Samonas Sound Therapy and the LiFT™ programme.

My introduction to sound therapy came via Sheila Frick and Therapeutic Listening®. I chose this method originally as it was being presented within a sensory integrative framework. As I was already using sensory integrative techniques with good results, it seemed to be the most appropriate next step. For a number of years I combined Therapeutic Listening® with other sensory integrative techniques and speech and language therapy, helping children to develop further and reaching even better levels than before. At this stage I believed that the children I was seeing were achieving their required levels.

However it was only when one or two new children didn't seem to be reaching the standards I thought they could achieve that I began to research other sound therapy programmes that I could add to our existing repertoire of programmes.

After much research and plenty of discussion with other therapists, I decided that my choice would be between the LiFT™ programme and the Tomatis method. Both programmes, which are highly regarded in the world of sound therapy, impressed me for a number of reasons: they are both intensive, primarily in-clinic programmes, comprising not only a receptive phase but an expressive phase using the microphone.

For me, as a speech and language therapist, the microphone is a fundamental component, as I know it has the capacity to open up children's speech, language and expressive abilities. Interestingly, these are the only two available sound therapy programmes that have an expressive phase. Most importantly, they were both reporting excellent results. I chose the LiFT™ programme, as the equipment offered a greater degree of versatility and mobility, allowing children to engage fully with their environment whilst listening.

10

Conclusion: other possible keys

Having worked with so many children with challenges over the past seventeen years, I know that music truly is the key to unlocking each child's potential. I see music as the key to the front door of the house, which brings you into the main area and opens the entire house to you. In a similar way music opens the neuropathways of the brain, unblocking the motorways so that skills can emerge successfully.

Sometimes, even though music is the main key, there can be other important keys, which can be beneficial if used prior to the introduction of the music, during the music programme or after the music. Just as there are other smaller rooms in the house, which help to add to the beauty of the entire building, there are other keys, which add to the child's skills by providing refinement and practice in specific areas. In my experience these other keys can be invaluable, particularly when used with music, in extending a child's potential even further. You will already be familiar with some of these keys, such as specific speech and language techniques, occupational therapy, physiotherapy and psychological approaches. There are other, lesser-known techniques that I want to make you aware of, so that you can investigate them further to see if they could possibly be a missing piece of the jigsaw for your child.

Allergy testing

We know that nutrition is critical for the optimal functioning of the brain and the nervous system. Of course the converse is also true: a deficiency of nutrients can set the scene for diminished or variable attention, listening, language and memory, resulting in the development of specific learning difficulties. Interestingly, children often have obvious physical signs that they are deficient in nutrients, have difficulty absorbing nutrients, or have allergies or intolerances. Pale skin or rashes, dark circles under the eyes, frequently runny or blocked nose, regular sore throats, sore ears, glue ear, build up of dark wax in the ear and regular chest infections are all signs to watch out for. This area ideally needs to be addressed prior to the start of listening therapy or at the very least at the point when therapy is starting for the best results. Otherwise we will be constantly working against the effects of the allergies or intolerances in the child's system and the results of the sound therapy will reflect this.

A good allergist or naturopath should identify any challenges that your child may be experiencing in this area and make appropriate recommendations.

Good reference books include *Optimum Nutrition for your Child* by Patrick Holford and Deborah Colson and *Gut and Psychology Syndrome* by Dr Natasha Campbell-McBride.

Homeopathy

This a form of medicine that involves treating a person with highly diluted substances with the aim of triggering the body's natural ability to heal. It is based on the principle of treating 'like with like': that a substance which causes symptoms when taken in large doses can be used in small amounts to treat symptoms. The principle of 'like with like' dates back to Hippocrates (460-377BC) but in its current form homeopathy has been widely used for more than two hundred years. In fact it was the kind of medicine most commonly practised by doctors in general medical practice before the use of pharmaceutical medicines became widespread in the 1920s. Interestingly it works not only on the physical level but on the mental and emotional level.

I came to learn about the far-reaching benefits of using homeopathy with both children and adults through a great homeopath and a good friend, Dr Goodwin McDonnell. I was intrigued by the results I saw that reduced children's anxiety levels, improved their levels of calmness, attention and concentration and enhanced their general health and wellbeing.

For further information: www.Irishhomeopathy.ie

Phytobiophysics

This is described as a revolutionary new concept/science approach whereby the energy of plants is used to harmonise and balance the disturbances of humanity on all levels of consciousness: spiritual, mental, emotional and physical. The philosophy of phytobiophysics was developed by Diana Mossop, who proposed that plants and trees have an extraordinary healing power. Building on the work of Dr Edward Bach, who demonstrated how many emotional states could be helped by using Bach flower remedies, Diana Mossop has extended the application of flower formulas to all types of illness. She is looking at how to improve the child's health and wellbeing to support and enhance brain function so that the child can have optimum learning ability. Although this is a relatively new approach, it appears to have potential.

For further information: www.phytob.com

Craniosacral Therapy

This is described as a subtle and profound form of healing that assists the body's ability to heal itself. Dr William Sutherland, an American osteopath, discovered that intrinsic movements of the bones of the skull can lead not only to better physical health but to improved mental and emotional health.

Craniosacral therapists believe that common problems with newborn babies, such as colic, sucking problems and respiratory difficulties, may be due to compression of the cranium arising from the birth. Examination of young children by craniosacral therapists may not only be curative but may be helpful in preventing problems later in life.

I generally refer for craniosacral work children who have had a traumatic birth history, who have a misshapen cranium or whose nervous system seems to require further integration.

My experience of craniosacral therapy has been positive but, as with any of the approaches described, it is important for it to be undertaken by a qualified and experienced paediatric practitioner.

For further information: www.IACST.com

Cognitive behaviour therapy

There are many excellent psychological approaches but one that stands out for me in my experience of working with children is cognitive behaviour therapy. In his book, *Flagging the Therapy,* Dr Harry Barry claims that no other form of therapy has such potential to revolutionise mental health in Ireland.

CBT is based on two simple concepts:

- Our thoughts influence our emotions, which in turn influence behaviour.
- It is not what happens to us in life that is important but how we choose to interpret it that matters.

Dr Gary O'Reilly, Deputy Director of the Doctoral Programme in Clinical Psychology at University College Dublin, has developed an excellent cognitive behaviour therapy workbook for children and adolescents. He describes it as a young person's guide to thinking straight and it is designed for use in a therapeutic context. I have found this programme invaluable when working with sensitive children and adolescents in helping them to develop healthy ways of thinking about challenging situations. This programme is available free of charge to clinics and qualified professionals from www.juvenilementalhealthmatters.com.

Selected bibliography

Ayres, A.J. (1972) *Sensory Integration and Learning Disorders.* Los Angeles: Western Psychological Services.

Barry, H. (2011) *Flagging the Therapy: Pathways Out of Depression and Anxiety.* Dublin: Liberties Press.

Borg, E. and S.A. Counter (1989, August) 'The Middle Ear Muscles'. *Scientific American*, 74-80.

Campbell-McBride, N. MD. (2004) *Gut and Psychology Syndrome.* Cambridge: Medinform Publishing.

Cool, S.J. (1987) 'A View from "Outside": Sensory Integration and Developmental Neurobiology'. *AOTA Sensory Integration Special Interest Section Newsletter*, 10 (2), 2-3.

Communicating Quality 2, 1996: *Professional Standards for Speech and Language Therapists.* Anna van der Gaag (ed.).

Cutler, Stevens-Dominguez and Peter Westby. (1992) 'Development of Self-regulation'. William, M.S. and S. Shellenberger (eds.) *How Does Your Engine Run? A Leader's Guide to the Alert Program™ for Self-regulation.* Albuquerque, New Mexico: TherapyWorks Inc.

Di Leo, J. (1970) *Young Children and Their Drawings.* New York: Brunner/Mozel, Inc.

Dunn, W. (1999) *Sensory Profile.* The Psychological Corporation, Harcourt Assessment Company.

Fisher, A. G., E.A. Murray and A.C. Bundy (eds.). (1994) *Sensory Integration : Theory and Practice.* Philadelphia: F.A. Davis.

Frick, S. (2006, 2009) *Listening with the Whole Body.* Madison, Wisconsin: Vitallinks.

Guitar, B. (1998) *Stuttering: An Integrated Approach to Its Nature and Treatment.* Baltimore, MD: Lippincott, Williams and Wilkins.

Harris, D.B. (1963) *Goodenough-Harris Drawing Test.* San Antonio, Texas: Psychological Corporation.

Holford, P. and D. Colson (2008). *Optimum Nutrition for Your Child.* London: Piatkus.

Irwin, A. (1988) *Stammering in Young Children.* London: Thorsons.

Kranowitz, C. (1996) *The Out-of-Sync Child.* New York: Perigee.

Madaule, P. (1989) *Left Out: The Rejection Complex of the Adopted.* Toronto: The Listening Centre.

Madaule, P. (1993) *When Listening Comes Alive.* Ontario: Moulin Publishing.

Madaule, P. (2000) *Listening Fitness Trainers' Manual.* Toronto: The Listening Centre.

Oetter, P., E. Richter and S. Frick. (1995) MORE: *Integrating the Mouth with Sensory and Postural Functions* (2nd edition). Hugo, Minnesota: PDP Press Inc.

O'Reilly, Dr G. *CBT Workbook for Children and Adolescents – A Young Person's Guide to Thinking Straight.* Available online from: http://www.juvenilementalhealthmatters.com.

Rustin, L., W. Botterill and E. Kelman. (1996) *Assessment and Therapy for Young Dysfluent Children: Family Interaction.* San Diego, California: Singular Publishing Group.

Ratey, J.J. (2002) *A User's Guide to the Brain: Perception, Attention and the Four Theatres of the Brain.* New York: Vintage.

Tallal, P., S. Miller and R. Fitch. (1993) 'Neurobiological Basis of Speech: A Case for the Pre-eminence of Temporal Processing'. P. Tallal, A.M. Galaburda, R.R. Llinas and C. Von Euler (eds.). *Temporal Information Processing in the Nervous System: Special Reference to Dyslexia and Dysphasia. Annals of the New York Academy of Sciences,* 682, 27-47.

Tallal, P. (1998) 'Language Learning Impairment: Integrating Research and Remediation'. *Scandinavian Journal of Psychology*, 39, 3, 197-199.

Tomatis, A. (1996) *The Ear and Language*. Ontario: Moulin Publishing.

Wilbarger, P. and J.L. Wilbarger. (1991) *Sensory Defensiveness in Children Aged 2-12: An Intervention Guide for Parents and Other Caretakers*. Santa Barbara, California: Avanti Educational Programs.

Index